CW00688403

The Sales
Training
Handbook

The Sales Training Handbook

52 Quick, Easy-to-Lead Mini-Seminars

Jeffrey L. Magee, Ph.D., CMC

McGraw-Hill

New York   Chicago   San Francisco   Lisbon
London   Madrid   Mexico City   Milan
New Delhi   San Juan   Seoul
Singapore   Sydney   Toronto

McGraw-Hill

A Division of The **McGraw·Hill** *Companies*

Copyright © 2001 by The McGraw-Hill Companies, Inc. All rights reserved. Printed in the United States of America. Except as permitted under the United States Copyright Act of 1976, no part of this publication may be reproduced or distributed in any form or by any means, or stored in a database or retrieval system, without the prior written permission of the publisher.

1 2 3 4 5 6 7 8 9 0   1PBT/1PBT   0 9 8 7 6 5 4 3 2 1

ISBN 0-07-137516-3

Printed and bound by Phoenix Book Technology

McGraw-Hill books are available at special quantity discounts to use as premiums and sales promotions, or for use in corporate training sessions. For more information, please write to the Director of Special Sales, Professional Publishing, McGraw-Hill, Two Penn Plaza, New York, NY 10121-2298. Or contact your local bookstore.

Important Guidelines for Photocopying or Downloading Pages from This Publication

Permission is granted free of charge to photocopy the "participation handout" pages of this publication, or to download and customize participant handouts from http://www.books.mcgraw-hill.com/training/download, for use in a training session. Only the original book purchaser conducting training sessions may make such photocopies or download these handouts. Under no circumstance is it permitted to sell or distribute on a commercial basis material reproduced from this publication. Except as expressly provided above, no part of this book may be reproduced or distributed in any form or by any means, or stored in a database or retrieval system, without the prior written permission of the publisher. Permission may be obtained by contacting

The McGraw-Hill Companies
Permissions Department, 9th Floor
Two Penn Plaza
New York, NY 10121-2298, U.S.A.

Telephone: 212-904-2574
Fax: 212-904-6285

 This book is printed on recycled, acid-free paper containing a minimum of 50% recycled, de-inked fiber.

Contents

SECTION THREE

Professional-Level Selling Skills

APPENDIX A

Professional Sales Skills Self-Assessment Inventory

Preface

The Sales Training Handbook is for sales managers and sales trainers who want to upgrade the skills of their salespeople and customer service representatives.

Most of the 52 mini-seminars presented in the book require just 15 to 20 minutes to deliver, so you can easily integrate training into existing meetings and engagements. You will learn how to train sales professionals in the basics of selling dynamics, in how to enhance dynamics, and more importantly, in how to sustain selling dynamics.

If you are a sales manager, sales trainer, small business owner, or coach, this book will provide you with specific skill development approaches. Each mini-seminar provides a brief presentation in the form of a lecturette, teaching points for maximum interaction with your sales professionals or sales team, and exercises or team activities for the participants. Because each mini-seminar is designed to provide your sales team with new insights through enhanced skill development, you and your sales team can benefit from using this guide immediately.

How to Use This Book

This book includes 52 training mini-seminars with individual lecturettes to assist you in preparing what to say to your sales team, class, or organization, as well as Activity Sheets that you can photocopy for all participants.

Now, in a few minutes daily or weekly, you can help your sales team to enhance their selling skills and increase their ability to interact with prospects or clients to achieve measurable results. The exercises in this book will:

• Ensure that consistent and easy learning takes place.

• Give you a turnkey approach to sales training.

• Allow for training to be easily integrated into meetings.

• Provide focused training on-the-go.

• Allow for progressive skill development year-round.

You and your sales staff can take one mini-seminar per week and make this a year-long affair. More ambitious groups may want to tackle the mini-seminars on a more frequent basis. Allow sufficient application time for each tool, and as a warm-up to each meeting, take a few minutes to debrief the previous mini-seminar's ideas in terms of how they have been used since they were presented. Allow time to discuss success stories and best practices.

Why This Book?

In today's fast-paced business world, sales professionals have limited presentation time with prospective customers and active customers. Their ability to maximize the sales opportunity is critical. This book helps the sales trainer, sales manager, and small business owner to facilitate controlled, systematic skill development that yields increased efficiency, producing greater sales and increased profitability for the organization.

It is critical that sales professionals and customer service representatives at the front line continually sharpen the tools of their craft. *The Sales Training Handbook* helps your sales professionals to compete head-to-head with other sales professionals who have enjoyed the luxury of attending a structured sales course for weeks, and to attain greater results than their colleagues. The 52 mini-seminars presented here provide the format to lead your team to success. They can be utilized to train individuals on a one-on-one basis, or as a group- or team-based intervention.

With more than two decades of experience as a sales professional, researcher, author, and performance coach, the author has participated in many sales training courses over the past decade, as a participant, a facilitator, or a course designer. The best of all of those courses has been put into this book for you and your sales team. The result is a series of easy-to-use training designs that you can facilitate with your sales team. Then, step aside and watch the **immediate results**!

The Sales
Training
Handbook

Training Your Team in the Five Basics of Selling

Objectives

1. To have participants identify the basic working knowledge needed by the sales professional and customer service representative.

2. To help salespeople practice describing what they have to offer.

Time Required

20–30 minutes

Materials Needed

- One copy of each of the four activity sheets for each participant

- A list of all the products or services that your organization or department offers

- A flip chart or whiteboard

Directions for the Trainer

1. Read the lecturette prior to your training session, and take notes so you can use it as the basis for your own comments to the group.

2. Start the training session by summarizing the lecturette for the group in your own words; then pass out the activity sheets.

3. Activity Sheet 1-A: Remind participants that it's important to have a practical working knowledge of what is offered by your organization or department. Make a competitive game of this exercise: Have participants complete this form in 60 seconds, to see how much each one knows. If they finish writing before the 60 seconds is up, ask them to sit in silence. After the allotted time, discuss what they have written down, identifying items as Claims, Facts or Features, and Benefit statements.

Mini-Seminar 1

Product IQ = Claims + Features + Benefits + Naildowns

Designing Your Position Statement

4. Activity Sheet 1-B: Now re-present the difference between a boastful claim and a basic fact or feature. Remind participants that it is the benefit that actually motivates a consumer to buy. Working individually or in small teams, have participants take one of the items from Activity Sheet 1-A and expand on it, describing its correlating benefits. Debrief this exercise to make sure that everyone understands the difference between a Claim, a Fact or Feature, and a Benefit. Refer to printed advertisements that your organization uses and analyze them to see how many make Claims, state Facts, and describe Benefits.

5. Activity Sheet 1-C: Explain how a Claim statement leads into a Fact or Feature statement, and then into a Benefit statement, and finally into a confirming question or Naildown statement. With the group, develop a list of suitable Naildown statements for every Benefit statement written or given in a sales presentation.

6. Activity Sheet 1-D: Have participants write a Position Statement—what they might say if asked, "What do you do?" Encourage them to develop a concise 60-second statement—(an elevator pitch).

LECTURETTE

Many sales professionals believe that bombarding the consumer with claims of greatness will earn them business. We see this in advertising, sales promotions, and Internet billboards, and we hear it from announcers on radio and television.

As you observe your colleagues, notice whether they speak in vague generalities of claims, using phrases like "We are the best" or "We have the biggest, newest, greatest, fastest, cheapest." Phrases containing the "est" words are typically claims, and those same claims could be made by your competition. Salespeople who make Claims hope that the consumer will accept those Claims without asking for verification.

Avoid using Claim statements in your presentations, as they can be turn-offs for the consumer. If a Claim is going to be made, then an associated fact statement must be offered in the same sentence. For example:

> "This widget is the best (Claim) in the market right now, because of its ABC Feature (Fact or Feature). It has been rated number one in value by *Consumer Reports*, so it offers the quality and reliability (Benefit) you desire."

The Claim ("best") is immediately associated with a specific Feature ("ABC") that is reinforced by an acknowledged third-party authority (*Consumer Reports*), and the Benefits presented are quality and reliability.

In many instances, baseless Claims are made by sales professionals who lack the working knowledge of the actual product or service that is necessary to accurately represent an organization. The more working knowledge a sales professional has of all the tangibles or intangibles offered by your organization—the specific facts or features—the better able he will be to point out the Benefits to the consumer.

Master sales professionals have an extensive working knowledge of what they represent and therefore of what they have to sell or offer. They have the ability to match up consumer needs with the solutions they offer by describing in detail the facts or features of the products or services they represent. The less working knowledge a sales professional has, the weaker his sales performance will be over time.

In making a simple presentation to a consumer, the sales professional may make a Claim to grab the consumer's attention ("We are the best"), but that Claim must then be immediately associated with an appropriate and corresponding Fact or Feature statement, and with a Benefit statement. It is the Benefit statement that ties the Fact or Feature statement to "What's in it for me?" from the buyer's perspective.

To ensure that the sales professional has correctly connected with what is important to and valued by the consumer, the sales professional finishes the presentation sequence (Product = Claim + Features + Benefit) with a corresponding Naildown statement that might sound like this:

> "And that is the level of quality and reliability that you want, isn't it?"

A Naildown (Product = Claim + Features + Benefit + Naildown) is a positive statement in the form of a confirming question directed toward the consumer to reinforce a key Fact or Feature presented and tie it to the appropriate Benefit.

Getting consumers involved in this process early and showing them how you can partner with them to solve their needs is a fast track to closing sales.

One way to determine whether a sales professional can engage in this most basic dialogue with a consumer is to find out how he responds when asked, "What do you do?" or "What makes your organization better than others?" I refer to the sales professional's response as his Position Statement. In other words, how do you position yourself when given the opportunity to gain another person's attention and interest?

A Position Statement must be very natural, simple, and powerful, so that you tell the other person just enough but not too much about who you are. It should be worded in such a way that it almost compels the listener to ask for more information. It should be an automatic response to anyone, anywhere, who asks, "So, what do you do?" Some professionals call this statement an elevator pitch. If you were on an elevator and had only a precious few seconds to answer that question, what would you say that would motivate the other person to get off the elevator with you and ask for more information?

A sales professional's first words create your first impression. Your Position Statement draws upon your basic working knowledge of what you offer: the features, the associated benefits, and how the benefits answer a need expressed by the other person. This is the foundation for selling success.

If I were selling skill development training sessions to a client, my Position Statement might sound like this:

> "I work with individuals who want to significantly increase their ability to interact with others effectively, resulting in better account relationships and more profitable sales!"

If someone is serious about wanting to improve his sales effectiveness, he is almost sure to follow up by asking me more questions. I now have an opportunity to draw upon my basic working knowledge to serve his needs, and that results in a sale!

Remember, a Claim is an assertion; a Fact or Feature is a tangible expression of what something does or is; a Benefit is how a Feature helps someone; and a Naildown is a statement that seeks confirmation from the other party that the Claim + Feature + Benefit are important.

Strong sales professionals have a highly developed working knowledge of what they offer and who they are.

ACTIVITY SHEET 1-A
BASIC PRODUCT KNOWLEDGE INDEX:
WHAT DO "I" OFFER?

In sixty seconds (you may invest additional time on your own after the seminar), identify your working product or service knowledge by listing as many products or services as possible that you offer:

_____ _____ _____

_____ _____ _____

_____ _____ _____

_____ _____ _____

_____ _____ _____

_____ _____ _____

_____ _____ _____

_____ _____ _____

_____ _____ _____

_____ _____ _____

_____ _____ _____

_____ _____ _____

_____ _____ _____

_____ _____ _____

_____ _____ _____

_____ _____ _____

_____ _____ _____

_____ _____ _____

_____ _____ _____

Copyright McGraw-Hill 2001. Original purchasers of this book are permitted to photocopy or customize this page by downloading it from www.books.mcgraw-hill.com/training/download. The document can then be opened, edited, and printed using Microsoft Word or other word processing software.

ACTIVITY SHEET 1-B
BASIC PRODUCT KNOWLEDGE INDEX:
PRODUCT IQ = CLAIM + FEATURE + BENEFIT.

In sixty seconds (you may invest additional time on your own after the completion of the seminar), identify your working product or service knowledge by examining one Fact or Feature of a single product you offer. Start by identifying a typical Claim that might be used in association with that Fact or Feature, and then list as many Benefits as you can that could be associated with it:

1. Identify one product or service:

    _____

2. Identify one Claim statement that could be used in association with this product or service:

    _____

3. Identify one Fact or Feature about that product or service:

    _____

4. Now brainstorm all the motivating Benefits associated with that Fact or Feature. Because no one Benefit statement will work with all consumers, having a ready arsenal of responses can assist you in closing a sale.

    _____ _____ _____

    _____ _____ _____

    _____ _____ _____

    _____ _____ _____

    _____ _____ _____

    _____ _____ _____

    _____ _____ _____

    _____ _____ _____

    _____ _____ _____

Copyright McGraw-Hill 2001. Original purchasers of this book are permitted to photocopy or customize this page by downloading it from www.books.mcgraw-hill.com/training/download. The document can then be opened, edited, and printed using Microsoft Word or other word processing software.

ACTIVITY SHEET 1-C
BASIC PRODUCT KNOWLEDGE INDEX:
PRODUCT IQ = CLAIM + FEATURE + BENEFIT + NAILDOWN.

In sixty seconds (you may invest additional time on your own after the seminar), identify your working product or service knowledge by examining one Fact or Feature of a single product you offer.

Take that Fact or Feature, its typical Claim, a related Benefit statement, and now develop a powerful Naildown statement (remembering that a Naildown statement is a positively framed question to solicit what you feel to be important in addressing their needs and is in fact appreciated and valued by the consumer):

1. Identify one product or service:

   _____

2. Identify one Claim statement that could be used in association with this product or service:

   _____

3. Identify one Fact or Feature about that product or service:

   _____

4. Identify one Benefit statement relating to the Fact or Feature:

   _____

5. Now brainstorm a list of powerful Naildown statements:

   _____

   _____

   _____

Copyright McGraw-Hill 2001. Original purchasers of this book are permitted to photocopy or customize this page by downloading it from www.books.mcgraw-hill.com/training/download. The document can then be opened, edited, and printed using Microsoft Word or other word processing software.

ACTIVITY SHEET 1-D
POSITION STATEMENT

In just a few seconds time, you must be able to tell someone else, who doesn't know or understand you, what it is that you do. Call this opening statement of excitement and intrigue your Position Statement.

Develop your Position Statement by first listing power words that best describe what it is that you do or offer. Then examine those words for likeness and similarities and draft one simple sentence. Review the sentence and commit it to memory, so that you can recite it at a moment's notice.

First, list as many words as you can that describe who you are or what you do professionally:

_____   _____   _____

_____   _____   _____

_____   _____   _____

_____   _____   _____

_____   _____   _____

_____   _____   _____

_____   _____   _____

Now complete the following sentence:

My name is _____, I work with individuals (or businesses)

that _____

_____

_____

Copyright McGraw-Hill 2001. Original purchasers of this book are permitted to photocopy or customize this page by downloading it from www.books.mcgraw-hill.com/training/download. The document can then be opened, edited, and printed using Microsoft Word or other word processing software.

Objectives

1. To have participants identify why they personally believe in what they represent.

2. To have participants identify reasons why they as individuals are excited about what they have to offer.

Time Required

15–20 minutes

Materials Needed

- One copy of each of the two activity sheets for each participant

- A flip chart or whiteboard

Directions for the Trainer

1. Read the lecturette prior to your training session, and take notes so you can use it as the basis for your own comments to the group.

2. Start the training session by summarizing the lecturette in your own words for the group; then pass out the activity sheets.

3. Activity Sheet 2-A: Give participants 2 to 3 minutes to complete this form. Next, ask them to place a check mark next to their most resounding entry. Then debrief as a group, allowing participants to share what they placed check marks next to. You may want to start the dialogue by sharing one of your own reasons!

4. Discuss with the group why some of the reasons are so moving and how they influence our ability to engage people and sell our products or services.

5. Activity Sheet 2-B: Ask participants to write about "how" and "why" their most resounding reasons matter. Then discuss how those reasons influence their overall sales ability.

Mini-Seminar 2

Why Do "I" Care?: Defining Your Passion and Personal Buy-In Factor

LECTURETTE

The ability of a sales professional to believe in what she represents has a direct impact on how others perceive her. When a sales professional buys in to what she represents, that has a direct impact on her sales effectiveness. Studies indicate that successful sales agents have a firm belief in what they do and what they represent.

Knowing why one cares can help you to deal with the negatives associated with sales.

Think about this for a moment. When you believe in something that you do, your passion for it grows. When your passion grows, then your motivation grows. And, when your motivation grows, your buy-in level is likely to become firm with conviction.

The ability of the sales professional or customer service representative to take care of an existing client significantly increases her sales effectiveness with that customer. More than any other single factor, telegraphing and sharing your buy-in energy will help you to connect with the customer.

"Why do 'I' care?" is a question of passion, motivation, and conviction! The sales professional must understand the "why" of what she represents and the "why" of her own buy-in before she can be expected to represent her company enthusiastically to the world. It's important to understand your unique buy-in reasons and learn how to share them with the world.

ACTIVITY SHEET 2-A
WHY DO "I" CARE?:
DEFINING YOUR PASSION AND PERSONAL BUY-IN FACTOR

List your reasons for doing what you do each professional day. Dig deep within and identify "why" you do what you do or "why" you believe the role you fill is valuable to another person or to society as a whole:

_____ _____ _____

_____ _____ _____

_____ _____ _____

_____ _____ _____

_____ _____ _____

_____ _____ _____

_____ _____ _____

_____ _____ _____

_____ _____ _____

_____ _____ _____

_____ _____ _____

_____ _____ _____

Copyright McGraw-Hill 2001. Original purchasers of this book are permitted to photocopy or customize this page by downloading it from www.books.mcgraw-hill.com/training/download. The document can then be opened, edited, and printed using Microsoft Word or other word processing software.

ACTIVITY SHEET 2-B
WHY DO "I" CARE?:
DEFINING YOUR PASSION AND PERSONAL BUY-IN FACTOR

Now identify the one most important entry from Activity Sheet 2-A, and write "why" that reason is so important and "how" it is inwardly motivating for you:

_____

_____

_____

_____

_____

_____

_____

_____

_____

_____

_____

_____

_____

_____

_____

_____

_____

_____

_____

_____

_____

_____

Copyright McGraw-Hill 2001. Original purchasers of this book are permitted to photocopy or customize this page by downloading it from www.books.mcgraw-hill.com/training/download. The document can then be opened, edited, and printed using Microsoft Word or other word processing software.

Objectives

1. To introduce participants to the five basic steps of selling.

2. To teach participants to identify where a given customer is in relationship to the five steps and to determine the most efficient way to progress to the next step.

Time Required

20–30 minutes

Materials Needed

• One copy of each of the six activity sheets for each participant

• A flip chart or whiteboard

Directions for the Trainer

1. Read the lecturette prior to your training session, and take notes so you can use it as the basis for your own comments to the group.

2. Start the training session by summarizing the lecturette in your own words for the group; then pass out the activity sheets.

3. Activity Sheet 3-A: Working individually or in small teams, have participants identify as many positive ways as they can to gain another person's favorable Attention. Debrief with the whole group, asking individuals or teams to share their best ideas.

   Activity Sheet 3-B: Working individually or in small teams, have participants identify as many interactive, open-ended questions as they can that allow the sales professional to identify the customer's Interest level. Debrief with the whole group, asking individuals or teams to share their best ideas.

Mini-Seminar 3

Identifying the Five Steps to Selling

Activity Sheet 3-C: Working individually or in small teams, have participants identify some of their best Presentation phrases for presenting a Claim + Feature + Benefit + Naildown. Debrief with the whole group, asking individuals or teams the share their best ideas.

Activity Sheet 3-D: Working individually or in small teams, have participants identify unique, powerful, and visual ways to communicate how the customer's life will be enhanced by your product or service, so as to create a Desire within the customer. Debrief with the whole group, asking individuals or teams to share their best ideas.

Activity Sheet 3-E: Working individually or in small teams, have participants identify easy ways to ask for the sale, listing questions that will Close the selling process and motivate the customer to accept the offer. Debrief with the whole group, asking individuals or teams to share their best ideas.

Activity Sheet 3-F: Working individually or in small teams, have participants put all five selling steps together in one clear, concise sequence. Have them role-play, saying the actual words to one another to hear how they sound. Let them practice how to respond if the planned words do not attain the desired goal. Debrief with the whole group, asking individuals or teams to share their best ideas.

LECTURETTE

Psychologists suggest that in the transaction of selling or buying, five essential steps must be taken by the sales professional. Sales professionals must understand each step, know how to accomplish the sequential objectives of each step, and know how to move the sales dialogue from one step to the next.

The five steps to selling are:

1. Attention,

2. Interest,

3. Presentation,

4. Desire,

5. Close.

"Attention" means getting the prospect's attention, despite any distractions or preoccupation, so that the focus is on your product or service. Sales professionals need to identify polite, smooth phrases that can be used to grab a prospect's attention and move the conversation to the more important second step, Interest.

Once Attention has been attained, your job is to identify the needs of the prospect or customer and determine whether you can address those needs. In the critical Interest step of the sales process, you must invest ample time exploring the prospect's or customer's immediate needs and continual needs and the ways in which you can meet those needs.

The Interest step is the most important step to invest time in. This is the needs analysis phase of the conversational approach. Ask thoughtful questions that stimulate informational responses from prospects or customers. Take notes while the prospect is answering, so you can limit the number of interruptions. Some of the best Interest questions are open-ended questions that stimulate dialogue between you and the prospect or customer. Asking open-ended questions encourages the customer to open up and provide you with a quantity of information.

Once you have identified the needs of the prospect via the Interest step, it's time to make your best Presentation of the appropriate product or service for the customer. The Presentation is based upon the Claim + Feature + Benefit + Naildown sequence developed in Mini-Seminar 2. After the Presentation, move the sales conversation toward illustrating how the prospect or customer will benefit by proceeding with your recommendation. This helps to build a level of Desire within the customer for what you have to offer.

Sales professionals must understand how to ask for the order, or Close the sales process. This final step in the selling process depends on the ability and confidence of the sales professional. If you are spending undue time on this fifth step, you may not be investing enough time in step two, Interest.

The art of the Close is in gauging the level of receptiveness to buying of the prospect or customer. Ask questions that allow you the flexibility either to finalize the order or to digress if necessary. Focus on two types of closing questions:

1. Trial Closes are opinion-asking questions. They help you to determine the customer's readiness to making a buying decision. An example of a Trial Close is: "If you were to go with this style widget, would you want to place the order on account or pay cash?"

2. The Order Close seeks a commitment from the prospect or customer. This Close question is used when you are confident that the prospect or customer is ready to take ownership of your product or service. An example of an Order Close is:

   "If you will tell me the quantity you need, we will have those sent to you immediately."

Every sales transaction involves all five selling steps. The sales professional must be able to gauge how much time to invest in each step before moving to the next step.

ACTIVITY SHEET 3-A
ATTENTION

The purpose of an effective Attention statement is to draw the prospect's or customer's attention to you and thus allow you the opportunity to engage them in the selling process. Write as many effective and natural sounding Attention statements as you can:

_____

_____

_____

_____

_____

_____

_____

_____

_____

_____

_____

_____

_____

_____

_____

_____

_____

_____

_____

_____

_____

_____

Copyright McGraw-Hill 2001. Original purchasers of this book are permitted to photocopy or customize this page by downloading it from www.books.mcgraw-hill.com/training/download. The document can then be opened, edited, and printed using Microsoft Word or other word processing software.

ACTIVITY SHEET 3-B
INTEREST

The Interest step is the *needs-analysis* phase of the selling process. Develop a series of open-ended questions that will draw a prospect or customer into a conversation and allow you to gather quality information about the person's immediate and on-going needs:

_____

_____

_____

_____

_____

_____

_____

_____

_____

_____

_____

_____

_____

_____

_____

_____

_____

_____

_____

_____

_____

_____

_____

_____

_____

_____

Copyright McGraw-Hill 2001. Original purchasers of this book are permitted to photocopy or customize this page by downloading it from www.books.mcgraw-hill.com/training/download. The document can then be opened, edited, and printed using Microsoft Word or other word processing software.

ACTIVITY SHEET 3-C
PRESENTATION

The Presentation step requires that the sales professional maintain control, so as not to oversell the prospect or customer. The purpose of the Presentation step is to present a complete response to the need you have identified through the *needs-analysis* or Interest phase. Write a series of complete responses to a prospect or customer's need. (Remember: Product or Service Presentation = Claim + Feature + Benefit + Naildown.)

_____

_____

_____

_____

_____

_____

_____

_____

_____

_____

_____

_____

_____

_____

_____

_____

_____

_____

_____

_____

_____

_____

_____

Copyright McGraw-Hill 2001. Original purchasers of this book are permitted to photocopy or customize this page by downloading it from www.books.mcgraw-hill.com/training/download. The document can then be opened, edited, and printed using Microsoft Word or other word processing software.

ACTIVITY SHEET 3-D
DESIRE

Prospects or customers don't typically make buying decisions if they are not amply motivated or do not Desire the item being offered. Write examples of conversational ways to build Desire in your Presentation to a prospect or customer.

_____

_____

_____

_____

_____

_____

_____

_____

_____

_____

_____

_____

_____

_____

_____

_____

_____

_____

_____

_____

_____

_____

_____

Copyright McGraw-Hill 2001. Original purchasers of this book are permitted to photocopy or customize this page by downloading it from www.books.mcgraw-hill.com/training/download. The document can then be opened, edited, and printed using Microsoft Word or other word processing software.

ACTIVITY SHEET 3-E
CLOSE

The purpose of the Close step is to do exactly that—close the selling process by asking for the order. There are two ways to approach the Close.

First, if you sense that the prospect or customer is warm to your offer (Presentation) but you are not sure the person is ready to buy, use a Trial Close question. The purpose of this type of question is to seek the customer's opinion of (not commitment to) your offer. Write several Trial Close questions for a typical Presentation that you might make:

_____

_____

_____

_____

_____

_____

_____

_____

_____

_____

Second, if you are confident that your Presentation has answered the customer's needs and that the customer is ready to buy, use an Order Close question, which seeks a commitment from the customer. Write a few Order Close questions for a typical Presentation that you might make:

_____

_____

_____

_____

_____

_____

_____

_____

_____

Copyright McGraw-Hill 2001. Original purchasers of this book are permitted to photocopy or customize this page by downloading it from www.books.mcgraw-hill.com/training/download. The document can then be opened, edited, and printed using Microsoft Word or other word processing software.

ACTIVITY SHEET 3-F
THE FIVE STEPS TO SELLING

Now, put it all together in a mock selling situation. Complete this activity sheet as if you were making a sales presentation to a typical prospect or customer of your organization.

Attention:

_____

_____

_____

Interest:

_____

_____

_____

Presentation:

_____

_____

_____

Desire:

_____

_____

_____

Trial Close:

_____

_____

_____

Close:

_____

_____

_____

Copyright McGraw-Hill 2001. Original purchasers of this book are permitted to photocopy or customize this page by downloading it from www.books.mcgraw-hill.com/training/download. The document can then be opened, edited, and printed using Microsoft Word or other word processing software.

Objectives

1. To have participants learn how to blend the five selling steps into their existing sales approach or selling cycle.

2. To have participants understand that there is a system to successful selling and a specific chronology for that process to follow. Based upon this enhanced understanding, the sales professionals should be able to benchmark their performance against this system to determine where they are in the sales cycle at any given time, gauge whether they have spent ample time on that step, and advance smoothly to the next step.

Time Required

10–15 minutes

Materials Needed

- One copy of the activity sheet for each participant

- A flip chart or whiteboard

Directions for the Trainer

1. Read the lecturette prior to your training session, and take notes so you can use it as the basis for your own comments to the group.

2. Start the training session by summarizing the lecturette in your own words for the group; then pass out the activity sheets.

3. Activity Sheet 4-A: Have participants work individually to complete the Activity Sheet, listing present actions and proposed enhanced actions for each step. Debrief with the whole group, asking individuals to share their best ideas.

Mini-Seminar 4

Building Your Sales Presentation Around the Five Steps

LECTURETTE

Psychologists suggest that there are five essential steps to the process or cycle of selling. Whether the selling is done face-to-face, in a group presentation, over the telephone, via e-mail, or through direct mail, there are specific objectives for each step in the selling process.

Depending upon your level of proficiency, you may need to focus more energy on one step or another. And, depending upon the needs of the prospect or customer, you may spend more or less time on a specific step in the selling cycle.

Remember the five steps:

Attention, Interest, Presentation, Desire, and Close.

If your sales conversation with the prospect or customer is effective, you will know when and how to interject an appropriate solution to the need of the prospect or customer that you have discovered. Remember the elements that a complete Presentation includes:

Product or Service Recommendation = Claim + Feature + Benefit + Naildown

Some sales professionals have a tendency to invest too much time talking or visiting at step one, rather than establishing good rapport for a smooth transition to the second step, where you will identify the prospect's or customer's needs and level of interest in what you have to offer. It is important to accomplish step one quickly and move into step two, because with effective questioning in step two, you will find out how much or how little information to provide in step three.

Build powerful Claim + Feature + Benefit + Naildown statements into your response in step three. Become adept at effectively communicating the gains the customer will realize by accepting your offer. Many sales professionals fail to accomplish this valuable step; but building the want (or Desire) in the mind of the prospect or customer works to seal the customer's mental acceptance of your offer.

If you follow the sequence of the five steps to selling, you will successfully Close and gain the business.

ACTIVITY SHEET 4-A
BUILDING YOUR SALES PRESENTATION AROUND
THE FIVE STEPS

PARTICIPANT'S HANDOUT

Identify a selling situation that you will face today (face-to-face, group, e-mail, letter, or telephone) and identify how you would have facilitated that selling cycle prior to this seminar. Then edit that process using today's ideas, to see if you can improve any step. When you have completed the editing process, pair off with a colleague and trade ideas on both of your presentations.

Step One = _____:

_____

_____

_____

Step Two = _____:

_____

_____

_____

Step Three = _____:

_____

_____

_____

Step Four = _____:

_____

_____

_____

Step Five = _____:

_____

_____

_____

What adjustments would you make as a result of what you learned in today's seminar?

_____

_____

_____

_____
_____

Copyright McGraw-Hill 2001. Original purchasers of this book are permitted to photocopy or customize this page by downloading it from www.books.mcgraw-hill.com/training/download. The document can then be opened, edited, and printed using Microsoft Word or other word processing software.

Objectives

1. To have participants recognize the powerful positive and negative effects of one's attitude on the selling process.

2. To teach participants how to maintain a positive attitude at all times and within each of the five selling steps.

3. To teach participants how to reframe negative attitudes as positive attitudes.

Time Required

20–30 minutes

Materials Needed

- One copy of each of the five activity sheets for each participant

- A flip chart or whiteboard

Directions for the Trainer

1. Read the lecturette prior to your training session, and take notes so you can use it as the basis for your own comments to the group.

2. Activity Sheet 5-A: Have each participant complete this form as quickly as possible to gain a more accurate emotion-based response as to how each occurrence would influence them to behave. If some finish writing before 60 seconds is up, ask them to sit in silence. Debrief by asking some of the participants to share their responses and the reasons for those responses before beginning your session.

3. Start the training session by summarizing the lecturette for the group in your own words; then pass out the remaining activity sheets.

Mini-Seminar 5

The Impact of Attitude on Sales Performance

4. Activity Sheet 5-B: Working individually or in small teams, have participants complete this form in 60 seconds. Make this a healthy competition among participants. Debrief by asking some of the participants to share their responses.

5. Activity Sheet 5-C: Now re-present the five selling steps and have each participant or small team identify constructive Positive Attitudinal Responses for each step. Debrief by asking how this can be accomplished and why it is in the best interest of sales professionals to do so.

6. Activity Sheet 5-D: Have each participant develop an action plan for maintaining a positive attitude toward selling. Also, have participants work as a sales team to develop a list of action steps everyone can commit to that will create an atmosphere for positive energies.

7. Activity Sheet 5-E: Have each participant inventory the people at work and home who are the closest to them daily and who influence their daily behaviors and attitudes. Then have participants identify types of people who are not in their inventories but could be, and who would help stimulate positive mind-sets or attitudes.

LECTURETTE

In 1910, Professor William James of Harvard University first recognized scientifically that for all of the differences among human beings, we each maintain 100 percent control over one factor in our lives. Many denounced what he reported and many disliked the label affixed to it. In the 1940s and 1950s, another American psychological giant, B.F. Skinner, conducted additional studies to determine whether James's findings were accurate; Skinner verified the earlier results. Again, others refuted the findings based on a dislike of either the two individuals or their studies. Ironically, the opposition was actually validating the findings. Today, the torch is carried by Dr. Albert Ellis.

With nearly 100 years of scientific research and data, it is amazing that so many people still challenge the findings. What were the findings? What distinguishes humans from other living beings is that we each have the ability to control our own minds, and our minds dictate our behavior. Another way of saying it is:

> "Attitude is ... the voices in our head; it is how we talk to ourselves, which influences how we will either respond (logic based) or react (emotion based)."

Professional Selling Power magazine, a staple among professional salespeople, reports that a sales professional can increase his selling proficiency 100 percent:

1. Having a selling system that works can increase sales effectiveness and net results by as much as 30 percent.

2. Following a selling program or procedure can increase selling effectiveness and net results by as much as 20 percent.

3. Maintaining a positive mind-set or attitude has an impact on your perspective and personality and can influence your selling effectiveness and net results by as much as 50 percent.

As a sales professional, you can increase your effectiveness and bottom-line results by removing all barriers to a positive attitude and creating an atmosphere that is most conducive to positive behaviors.

Can you recognize how you feel emotionally and intellectually after a great sale? How do you feel when you feel appreciated by others? How do you tend to act in those situations?

How you mentally see yourself or a situation sets off a series of mental dialogues with yourself (internal voices). These dialogues stimulate you to act or react as you do. Look at this phenomenon further. Consider how you get to work each day, who you interact with at work, and what tasks you work on first and last each day. Psychology refers to each of these as a stimulant. It is the stimulants you are subjected to that influences your mind-set. How you interpret a stimulant influences your thinking, and that in turn influences your behavioral response or reaction.

Sales professionals must realize that how they see things and interpret things influences their ability to effectively execute each of the five steps to selling. Studies show that:

Activating Event + Attitude (mind-set or interpretation of event) =
Outcome

To ensure greater positive outcomes, the sales professional must realize that how you manage the stimulant will influence both your mind-set and the prospect's or customer's mind-set.

One powerful way to recognize this is to inventory who you hold in your inner circle of confidence. Master sales professionals can trace their successes to many influencers, and among those are the positive-minded individuals they interact with, both at work and at home.

In the 1940s and 1950s, one of the most powerful sales professionals in America was an insurance salesman named W. Clement Stone, who went on to head a multibillion-dollar firm. Mr. Stone called these positive people influencers his "Mental Board of Directors."

Remember the childhood adage:
Birds of a feather flock together!

A positive attitude can enhance an already successful day and neutralize a poor day. Attitude influences the performance of every sales professional.

ACTIVITY SHEET 5-A
THE IMPACT OF ATTITUDE ON SALES PERFORMANCE

For each entry, write what you would say or do immediately if that situation occurred.

You awaken late: _____

_____

Someone fails to forward a message to you in a timely manner: _____

_____

You can't find your home or car keys: _____

_____

You spend a significant amount of time talking with a prospect or customer in expectation of making a sale, and then find out that the person is merely looking today: _____

_____

You are with a prospect or customer and another prospect or customer telephones for you; you are unable to take that phone call: _____

_____

You are driving down the roadway and another commuter passes you, then cuts in front of you; the driver makes an unflattering hand gesture: _____

_____

You are about to leave the office for the day and a prospect or customer contacts you: _____

_____

Copyright McGraw-Hill 2001. Original purchasers of this book are permitted to photocopy or customize this page by downloading it from www.books.mcgraw-hill.com/training/download. The document can then be opened, edited, and printed using Microsoft Word or other word processing software.

ACTIVITY SHEET 5-B
THE IMPACT OF ATTITUDE ON SALES
PERFORMANCE

Professionally speaking, identify as many things as possible that you can do daily to reinforce a positive mind-set or attitude or bounce back from a negative mind-set or attitude:

Ways to Maintain the Positive

1. _____
2. _____
3. _____
4. _____
5. _____
6. _____
7. _____
8. _____
9. _____
10. _____
11. _____
12. _____
13. _____
14. _____
15. _____
16. _____
17. _____
18. _____
19. _____
20. _____
21. _____
22. _____
23. _____
24. _____
25. _____
26. _____
27. _____
28. _____
29. _____
30. _____

Ways to Bounce Back from the Negative

1. _____
2. _____
3. _____
4. _____
5. _____
6. _____
7. _____
8. _____
9. _____
10. _____
11. _____
12. _____
13. _____
14. _____
15. _____
16. _____
17. _____
18. _____
19. _____
20. _____
21. _____
22. _____
23. _____
24. _____
25. _____
26. _____
27. _____
28. _____
29. _____
30. _____

Copyright McGraw-Hill 2001. Original purchasers of this book are permitted to photocopy or customize this page by downloading it from www.books.mcgraw-hill.com/training/download. The document can then be opened, edited, and printed using Microsoft Word or other word processing software.

ACTIVITY SHEET 5-C
ATTITUDINAL RESPONSES TO THE FIVE STEPS
TO SELLING

Identify several things you can do to ensure that each of the five selling cycles is positive and constructive. Also, list corrective actions that can be taken at each step to convert a negative mind-set or attitude back to a positive one.

Attention:

_____

_____

_____

_____

Interest:

_____

_____

_____

_____

Presentation:

_____

_____

_____

_____

Desire:

_____

_____

_____

_____

Close:

_____

_____

_____

_____

Copyright McGraw-Hill 2001. Original purchasers of this book are permitted to photocopy or customize this page by downloading it from www.books.mcgraw-hill.com/training/download. The document can then be opened, edited, and printed using Microsoft Word or other word processing software.

ACTIVITY SHEET 5-D
PROFESSIONAL ENVIRONMENT ATTITUDE ADJUSTER

Identify specific action plans for each situation to stimulate positive focus and a positive mind-set.

1. On the way to work each day, I should be thinking about and talking to myself about: _____

    _____

    _____

    _____

2. Upon arriving at work each day, I should immediately:_____

    _____

    _____

    _____

3. Before returning a phone call or e-mail to someone, I should: _____

    _____

    _____

    _____

4. Immediately after making a sale (Close step), I should: _____

    _____

    _____

    _____

5. Immediately after not making a sale (Close step), I should: _____

    _____

    _____

    _____

6. Immediately after leaving a meeting, I should: _____

    _____

    _____

    _____

7. On my way home at the end of a sales day, I should: _____

    _____

    _____

    _____

Copyright McGraw-Hill 2001. Original purchasers of this book are permitted to photocopy or customize this page by downloading it from www.books.mcgraw-hill.com/training/download. The document can then be opened, edited, and printed using Microsoft Word or other word processing software.

ACTIVITY SHEET 5-E
PEOPLE INFLUENCERS IN YOUR LIFE:
YOUR PERSONAL BOARD OF DIRECTORS

PARTICIPANT'S
HANDOUT

Identify the specific people influencers at work and home who you tend to interact with most and whose views and opinions you hold in high regard.

1. At work, these are the people who influence me: _____

_____

_____

_____

_____

_____

_____

_____

_____

2. Some of the types of people I don't have in my inner circle of influencers but who would assist me in attaining the next level of effectiveness in life are: _____

_____

_____

_____

_____

_____

_____

_____

_____

_____

Copyright McGraw-Hill 2001. Original purchasers of this book are permitted to photocopy or customize this page by downloading it from www.books.mcgraw-hill.com/training/download. The document can then be opened, edited, and printed using Microsoft Word or other word processing software.

Objectives

1. To have participants understand the importance of a powerful positive start through gaining attention effectively, rather than visiting.

2. To have participants recognize ways to establish rapport with a prospect or customer and understand the relationship to the five selling steps.

Time Required

20–30 minutes

Materials Needed

- One copy of each of the two activity sheets for each participant

- A flip chart or whiteboard

Directions for the Trainer

1. Read the lecturette prior to your training session, and take notes so you can use it as the basis for your own comments to the group.

2. Start the training session by summarizing the lecturette in your own words for the group; then pass out the activity sheets.

3. Activity Sheet 6-A: Working individually or in small teams, have each participant complete the form. Make this a healthy competition among participants. Debrief by asking some of the participants to share their responses.

4. Activity Sheet 6-B: Develop the Question Bearing upon a Need attention-getting opening statement as an integral aspect of the five selling steps. Have the participants role-play their statements with partners. Debrief the group on the usage of this statement in selling situations and its usefulness in gaining immediate interest as an Attention step.

Mini-Seminar 6

Attention: How to Gain a Favorable Start

LECTURETTE

Knowing how to gain a positive, favorable start in the selling cycle is critical for maximizing time and increasing sales volume. Sales professionals must understand the difference between a "professional visitor" and a "professional salesperson."

The Attention step in selling is analogous to taking time to establish a solid foundation upon which to build a home. However you go about establishing rapport and building a relationship of trust, you are in essence gaining the prospect's or customer's favorable Attention.

Some sales professionals have not thought much about the power that effective Attention-getting plays in the overall sales process. Others fall into a routine sales opener that may not always work. Here are eight effective ways to gain immediate, favorable, and undistracted attention:

S   **Shocking Statement:** Start with a shocking statement that will grab attention.

H   **Handshake with Meaning:** Shake the other person's hand, solicit her name, and repeat it twice before letting go of her hand.

O   **Offer Something:** a gesture, gift, assistance, rebate, coupon, or information that will be valued by the receiver.

C   **Compliment:** Pay a sincere compliment; it could be something about clothing or accessories, conduct, reputation, accomplishment, or standing in the group.

K   **Know people by Name:** Use names early and often to establish rapport and make customers feel comfortable with you.

I   **Inquire:** Start with a positive question.

N   **Needs Analysis:** Offer a needs analysis or your observations of a correctable problem.

G   **Give a Gift:** Offer something of value from your organization as a gesture of welcome.

Another powerful Attention-getting conversational starter is to ask a Question **Bearing upon a Need** (known as a **QBN**). In order to use this technique effectively, the sales professional must have working knowledge of what you represent (see Mini-Seminar 1), understand the five selling steps (see Mini-Seminars 3 and 4), and know the typical customer served by the organization and what the usual needs are.

A QBN is a positively framed question that is tied to a statement designed to solicit agreement from the prospect to continue with the sales dialogue.

The architecture of a QBN is this:

> "If there were a way to _____ [Insert the perceived need of the customer.], would that be of interest to you?

"The reason I ask is that _____ [Insert your solution to the perceived need.] Perhaps we can do the same for you. In order to determine if we can, may I ask you a few questions?"

A completed QBN might sound like this:

"If there were a way to increase the effectiveness of your sales team, would that be of interest to you?"

"The reason I ask is that we have developed a selling system and training program that has significantly helped thousands of organizations to increase their sales effectiveness and overall profitability. Perhaps we could do the same for you. To determine if we can do so, may I ask you some additional questions?" (The last question takes you directly into step two of the selling process, with the customer's permission and undivided Attention.)

If properly set up, this Attention-getter can pull the prospect or customer into your dialogue quickly and allow you to move to step two of the selling process.

Whether you use a SHOCKING opening statement or a QBN, the objective is to determine whether your prospect or customer has an interest in continuing the selling dialogue. Gaining someone's Attention serves as the *attraction* phase to selling.

ACTIVITY SHEET 6-A
ATTENTION: HOW TO GAIN A FAVORABLE START

Identify ways that you can put each of the Attention-getting techniques to use:

Shocking Statement: _____

_____

Handshake and Get the Name: _____

_____

Offer Something: _____

_____

Compliment: _____

_____

Know By Name: _____

_____

Inquiring Question: _____

_____

Needs Analysis Offer: _____

_____

Give (gift) Something: _____

_____

Copyright McGraw-Hill 2001. Original purchasers of this book are permitted to photocopy or customize this page by downloading it from www.books.mcgraw-hill.com/training/download. The document can then be opened, edited, and printed using Microsoft Word or other word processing software.

ACTIVITY SHEET 6-B
ATTENTION: HOW TO GAIN A FAVORABLE START

Complete the following Attention-getting opener using a Question Bearing upon a Need. Identify a typical prospect or customer you serve and identify a product or service that you are familiar with for the role-play exercise.

Step One:

Typical Prospect or Customer: _____

Product or Service You Will Represent: _____

Step Two:

"Mr. or Ms. Customer, if there were a way to _____

_____

_____

_____, would that be of interest to you?"

Step Three:

"The reason I mention that is _____

_____

_____

_____.

Perhaps we can do the same for you. May I ask you a few questions?"

Copyright McGraw-Hill 2001. Original purchasers of this book are permitted to photocopy or customize this page by downloading it from www.books.mcgraw-hill.com/training/download. The document can then be opened, edited, and printed using Microsoft Word or other word processing software.

Objectives

1. To have participants understand the importance of the second step of the selling process, the needs analysis or Interest of the prospect or customer.

2. To empower the sales professional with comfortable conversational ways to engage the prospect or customer in a controlled dialogue to determine immediate and potential needs the salesperson can fulfill.

3. To have sales professionals recognize that this is the step in the selling process in which they should invest the most time. If they spend enough time here asking great questions, then the last three steps in the selling process will flow smoothly.

Time Required

20–30 minutes

Materials Needed

- One copy of each of the two activity sheets for each participant

- A flip chart or whiteboard

Directions for the Trainer

1. Read the lecturette prior to your training session, and take notes so you can use it as the basis for your own comments to the group.

2. Start the training session by summarizing the lecturette in your own words for the group; then pass out the activity sheets.

3. Activity Sheet 7-A: Working individually or in small teams, have each participant complete the form. Make this a healthy competition among participants. Debrief by asking some of the participants to share their responses.

Mini-Seminar 7

Interest: How to Capture It

4. Activity Sheet 7-B: Develop a series of specific engagement questions with participants for your primary products or services in the market right now, taking into account some of the barriers participants are currently encountering. Debrief the group on the usage of these questions and how they can benefit by becoming more involved with their prospects or customers in the critical second step of the selling process—Interest.

LECTURETTE

The difference between a veteran sales professional and a rookie can be observed in how the veteran engages prospects or customers by asking powerful questions designed to pull them into the selling dialogue. The answers to those questions help the sales professional determine the customer's exact needs and how the salesperson can meet those needs.

Many times you may notice that you are in a hurry to arrive at the Presentation step of the selling process without thoroughly identifying the potential buyer's needs or ability to purchase the solution that you have to offer.

Knowing how to gain the confidence of that other person and ask relevant, thoughtful questions that appear to be conversational takes work. Your job requires that you know how to accomplish this on a regular basis.

The questions you ask to identify the customer's Interest level in your product or service organization, or the sales professional themselves, should be open-ended in nature, to draw out the customer and provide a volume of initial information. As the conversation continues, begin to tighten up the questions (transition from open-ended to closed-ended questions) and seek qualifying information, to determine how best to meet the customer's needs.

Open-ended questions seek to solicit data and get the customer to participate in the selling process. Open-ended questions can't be answered with a single word, and typically begin with:

Who

What

When

Where

Why or

How

These question starters can be prefaced to solicit limited amounts of information. The preface directs the customer to provide precise and specific information. At times you'll need to follow up an open-ended questions with a closed-ended question, to confirm or get clarification of information.

Closed-ended questions are designed to get limited information or clarification of previous information. These questions are useful when a prospect or customer becomes too talkative. A prefaced, closed-ended question might begin with:

"Specifically, who [or what or when or where or why or how] . . .?"

Use questions strategically to *probe* for more information, to uncover additional selling opportunities, and to discover additional needs of the prospect or customer. *Evaluate* the types of questions that can be used to gather valuable information and the *chronology* in which they should be used to gain the greatest amount of information.

Questioning should also match the customer's level of interest, knowledge, and background. Remember, it is the purpose of the Interest step of the selling process to determine the specific needs of the prospect or customer, and then determine how you can meet those needs.

Within the scope of the questions you ask, three core questions must be included at this third step in the selling process. You must determine:

> Does the customer have a need for what you offer? If not, terminate the sales process!

> Does the customer have the capacity to pay for your product or service? If not, terminate the sales process!

> Does the customer have a time line for acquiring what you offer? If not, terminate the sales process!

At this step in the selling process, look for indications of the primary, immediate Interest levels of the potential buyer as well as indications of potential future Interest levels for additional selling opportunities. Use the words, "Mr. or Ms. Customer, what are you primarily interested in?"

By asking powerful, thoughtful questions, you will have a meaningful dialogue that will provide you with the information you need for the Presentation to your prospect or customer.

ACTIVITY SHEET 7-A
INTEREST: QUESTION SEQUENCE USING OPEN-ENDED
AND CLOSED-ENDED QUESTIONS

PARTICIPANT'S HANDOUT

Write open-ended Interest questions that could be used to stimulate a dialogue with a prospect or customer.

Step One:

Typical Prospect or Customer: _____

Product or Service You Will Present: _____

Step Two:

Who: _____

_____

_____?

What: _____

_____

_____?

When: _____

_____

_____?

Where: _____

_____

_____?

Why: _____

_____

_____?

How: _____

_____

_____?

Copyright McGraw-Hill 2001. Original purchasers of this book are permitted to photocopy or customize this page by downloading it from www.books.mcgraw-hill.com/training/download. The document can then be opened, edited, and printed using Microsoft Word or other word processing software.

ACTIVITY SHEET 7-B
INTEREST: QUESTION SEQUENCE USING OPEN-ENDED AND CLOSED-ENDED QUESTIONS

Write an Attention-getting opener with a Question Bearing upon a Need. Identify a customer you serve and identify a typical product or service that you are familiar with for the role-play exercise.

Step One:

Prospect or Customer: _____

Product or Service to Represent: _____

Some Challenges You Are Facing: _____

_____

Step Two:

Who: _____

_____

_____?

What: _____

_____

_____?

When: _____

_____

_____?

Where: _____

_____

_____?

Why: _____

_____

_____?

How: _____

_____

_____?

Copyright McGraw-Hill 2001. Original purchasers of this book are permitted to photocopy or customize this page by downloading it from www.books.mcgraw-hill.com/training/download. The document can then be opened, edited, and printed using Microsoft Word or other word processing software.

Objectives

1. To increase the efficiency of the participants in presenting a solution to a prospect or customer that meets a stated need.

2. To have participants understand the Presentation step of the selling process, using the sequence Product or Service = Claim + Feature + Benefit + Naildown.

Time Required

20–30 minutes

Materials Needed

- One copy of each of the two activity sheets for each participant

- A list of all the products or services your organization or department offers

- A flip chart or whiteboard

Directions for the Trainer

1. Read the lecturette prior to your training session, and take notes so you can use it as the basis for your own comments to the group.

2. Start the training session by summarizing the lecturette in your own words for the group; then pass out the activity sheets.

3. Activity Sheet 8-A: Have each participant complete the form, using several products or services as examples to ensure that they understand the entire process and that they complete each step. Debrief by asking for examples from the group.

   Listen for examples of Claims or incomplete Presentation steps. Remind participants that a complete Presentation is more than a Claim and contains the sequence: Claim + Feature + Benefit + Naildown.

Presentation: What's It All About?

4. Activity Sheet 8-B: Working individually or in small groups, have participants develop a complete Presentation sequence for your top revenue-generating products or services, using the most powerful Feature + Benefit + Naildown statements. Tie this exercise into the Question Bearing upon a Need technique presented in Mini-Seminar 6.

LECTURETTE

By asking powerful, thoughtful questions, you will be able to have a meaningful dialogue with your prospect or customer and make a more concise and effective Presentation. The sales professional's role is not only to present a solution for the needs uncovered in the Interest stage of the selling process. The Presentation sequence is designed to provide a complete response to a customer's needs:

Product or Service = Claim + Feature (Fact) + Benefit + Naildown

Learn to select from your mental inventory the appropriate product or service that will meet the needs of the prospect or customer that you uncovered in the Interest stage. Once that specific solution is presented, guide the conversational Presentation through all the parts of the formula (Product or Service = Claim + Feature [Fact] + Benefit + Naildown). Communicate the solution in such a way that it compels the listener to want your offer or solution immediately.

Some sales professionals have a tendency to oversell their solutions. Overpromising leads to prospect or customer skepticism (perhaps because it is often connected to under-delivering). While there may be an unlimited list of options, bells, whistles, and colors available, the prospect or customer only wants to hear about the combination that meets her needs. The sales professional must be confident that your solution will work and have the self-control to limit your remarks.

The Presentation should be given in such a manner that it yells to the prospect or customer, "I have been listening to your needs. Here is my customized response to you that speaks only to what you say you need!" Present the associated Features of a product or service that are most appropriate for that customer. Most products or services have many shared Features and Benefits. If you present all of them at once, then there are no additional dialogue points (ammunition) to present if the prospect or customer asks for more information.

A concise Presentation response to a prospect or customer might sound like this:

> "Based upon what we have discussed, I can suggest some ways in which we can meet your needs. Let me explain. The Widget-Master 2000 is the best option for your consideration, because it features the most recently approved and certified technology innovations, and that means you will have the most advanced and efficient widget in the market today. You do want the best technology in your environment, don't you?"

The power of the Presentation statement is that it starts with a Claim ("best option for your consideration"), then ties into a product solution ("Widget-Master 2000"), continues with a Feature statement("most recently approved and certified technology innovations"), then transitions into a Benefit statement ("advanced and efficient"), and concludes with a confirming Naildown question ("You do want the best technology in your environment, don't you?").

In a complete Presentation process, all the ingredients are communicated and conversational feedback is solicited to measure whether what was presented is valued by the prospect or consumer.

ACTIVITY SHEET 8-A
PRESENTATION: WHAT'S IT ALL ABOUT?

Develop a series of complete Presentation statements or responses for a product or service that you represent. Pick your two favorite or best-selling products or services and two of your more difficult products or services. Share your completed responses with your colleagues for feedback:

1. Favorite Product or Service: _____

   Claim: _____

   Feature or Fact Statement: _____

   Benefit Statement: _____

   Naildown Statement or Question: _____

2. Favorite Product or Service: _____

   Claim: _____

   Feature or Fact Statement: _____

   Benefit Statement: _____

   Naildown Statement or Question: _____

3. Challenge Product or Service: _____

   Claim: _____

   Feature or Fact Statement: _____

   Benefit Statement: _____

   Naildown Statement or Question: _____

4. Challenge Product or Service: _____

   Claim: _____

   Feature or Fact Statement: _____

   Benefit Statement: _____

   Naildown Statement or Question: _____

Copyright McGraw-Hill 2001. Original purchasers of this book are permitted to photocopy or customize this page by downloading it from www.books.mcgraw-hill.com/training/download. The document can then be opened, edited, and printed using Microsoft Word or other word processing software.

ACTIVITY SHEET 8-B
PRESENTATION: WHAT'S IT ALL ABOUT?

Develop a complete Presentation sequence, starting with a Question Bearing upon a Need for the product or service that provides the greatest revenue to your organization. Make your words as conversational and relaxed as possible. Share your completed responses with your colleagues for feedback:

Product or Service Selected: _____

_____

QBN: "If there were a way to, _____

_____

_____

would that be of interest to you?" (Assume a positive response and continue.) "The reason I ask is that we have been able to do that for many individuals. Perhaps we can do the same for you. To determine if we can, may I ask you a few questions?" (Assume that you have asked questions and now you are re-engaging the prospect or customer to make your Presentation. Continue your dialogue.)

Claim: _____

_____

_____

Feature or Fact Statement: _____

_____

_____

Benefit Statement: "Which means to you, _____

_____

_____

Naildown Statement or Question: "And, you do want _____

_____

_____

Copyright McGraw-Hill 2001. Original purchasers of this book are permitted to photocopy or customize this page by downloading it from www.books.mcgraw-hill.com/training/download. The document can then be opened, edited, and printed using Microsoft Word or other word processing software.

Objectives

1. To teach participants how to transfer their excitement and passion for their offer to the buyer.

2. To teach participants ways of generating the "want" for the offer within the buyer so the motivation to accept the offer grows.

Time Required

20–30 minutes

Materials Needed

- One copy of each of the three activity sheets for each participant

- A list of all the products or services your organization or department offers

- A flip chart or whiteboard

Directions for the Trainer

1. Read the lecturette prior to your training session, and take notes so you can use it as the basis for your own comments to the group.

2. Start the training session by summarizing the lecturette in your own words for the group; then pass out the activity sheets.

3. Activity Sheet 9-A: Have participants write out action-oriented solution scenarios for the prospect or customer, using any product or service they choose. Discuss what they have written. Debrief by asking some of the participants to share examples.

4. Activity Sheet 9-B: Now re-present the same exercise and have participants develop action-oriented solution scenarios for your leading product or service, using Word Picture statements. Debrief by asking some of the participants to share examples.

Mini-Seminar 9

Desire: Building the Emotional Want in Your Offer

5. Activity Sheet 9-C: Have individuals or small teams develop action-oriented Desire statements for any new product or service introductions in your organization. Debrief by asking some of the participants to share examples.

LECTURETTE

Typically, the weakest portion of any selling process is selling to the buyer's emotional needs and satisfying those needs and wants. If the sales professional speaks to the customer's Desires, then the want will be satisfied.

When addressing the Desire is built into the dialogue of the sales process, sales professionals experience less buying resistance and buyer's remorse. Buyer's remorse can result in returned purchases, apprehension about future purchases, and even refusal to consider future offers from the sales professional.

One powerful way to convey to potential buyers that their needs and wants are being addressed is to speak in terms of how they will benefit by accepting your sales offer. Move beyond the Benefit statement contained within the Presentation step of the selling process and share a word picture (words that convey a vivid picture) of the buyers using and enjoying the offer.

Desire is fed when potential buyers are led down a mental path picturing what their life will be like if they proceed with your offer. Your ability to convey the emotional aspects of a purchase depends upon your level of personal buy-in (see Mini-Seminar 2).

A Desire statement packed with vivid word pictures can span the entire sequence of Presentation elements (see Mini-Seminars 3, 4, and 8). It might sound like this:

> "Mr. or Ms. Prospect or Customer, if you proceed with the purchase of the Widget-Master 2000, here is what you will experience tomorrow. You will come into your office and look out at everyone's work stations as they turn on their computers. But instead of employees waiting in frustration for their systems to become operational, you will see employees' faces lighting up with smiles, because with the Widget-Master 2000, the systems will become operational instantly. Instead of colleagues being held up by slow systems, with the Widget-Master 2000 you will notice less stress and increased productivity."

Ensure that the word picture you have communicated (or verbally painted) is stimulating the buyer's Desire for your offer by following up with a Naildown confirming question. It might sound like this:

> "Is that the type of office environment that you would like to work in?"

If you have uncovered the customer's needs through engaging questioning at the Interest step of the selling process, and have done an effective job at the Presentation step, then the Desire step should be fun and automatic!

In order to do a thorough job of presenting an engaging and exciting word picture that stimulates the buyer's "want" and feeds the Desire for your offer, you must:

1. Have a thorough understanding of what products or services you represent.

2. Have engaged the prospect or customer effectively at the Attention selling step.

3. Have gotten permission from the prospect or customer to ask questions and have found out precisely what the buyer's Interest level is.

4. Have done a complete job at presenting a solution to the buyer in the Presentation selling step.

5. Personally believe in the Presentation sequence you have presented.

6. Believe in what you do.

7. Know how to weave words together in a way that allows the listener to see herself using and benefiting from the acceptance of your offer.

Some sales professionals become great storytellers, and the Desire step is a great place for those stories to be interjected. Avoid inserting stories in the beginning of the selling process; this can come across as overselling and may actually turn people off, resulting in lost business.

However, telling stories is a great way to illustrate your key points and enable prospects or customers to visualize what it could be like if they decide to partner with you as their solution provider. Many senior sales professionals excel at using stories to enhance Desire. Junior sales professionals can often benefit from pairing up with a veteran and listening to the colleague's sales presentations. Recall the scene with the two deer in the Disney movie *Bambi*: The junior sales professional (the fawn or doe, standing on the side of the babbling brook looking upward across the rolling green meadow to where the older buck stood looking down on them commandingly) may bring renewed energy and vigor to a team, and the veteran (the older buck) can share her knowledge, wisdom, and perspectives through colorful stories.

The most powerful word pictures are those that place the listener directly into the story, in the present tense. Desire is further stimulated by using words that capture the creative imagination of the listener (prospect or customer) and stimulate each of the bodily senses: sight, hearing, taste, touch, and smell.

Channel your sales energy in a controlled, systematic direction by thinking of selling as a science with very exacting steps.

ACTIVITY SHEET 9-A
DESIRE: BUILDING THE EMOTIONAL WANT IN YOUR OFFER
(FOR ANY PRODUCT OR SERVICE)

Choosing any product or service you represent, complete this conversation as if you have just finished the Presentation step of the selling process, using a word picture to construct a powerful Desire statement. (*Remember that your sentence should speak to as many sensations as possible—sight, hearing, taste, touch, and smell—to stimulate the listener to live your scenario.*)

"If you were to proceed with my recommendations, here is what you will experience:

_____

_____

_____

_____

_____

_____

_____

_____

_____

_____

_____

_____

_____

_____

_____

_____

_____

"Is that the scenario that you would like to experience?"

Copyright McGraw-Hill 2001. Original purchasers of this book are permitted to photocopy or customize this page by downloading it from www.books.mcgraw-hill.com/training/download. The document can then be opened, edited, and printed using Microsoft Word or other word processing software.

ACTIVITY SHEET 9-B
DESIRE: BUILDING THE EMOTIONAL WANT IN YOUR OFFER
(FOR YOUR LEADING PRODUCT OR SERVICE)

Choosing the leading product or service you represent, complete this conversation as if you have just finished the Presentation step of the selling process, using a word picture to construct a powerful Desire statement. (*Remember that your sentence should speak to as many sensations as possible—sight, hearing, taste, touch, and smell—to stimulate the listener to live your scenario.*)

"If you were to proceed with my recommendations, here is what you will experience:

_____

_____

_____

_____

_____

_____

_____

_____

_____

_____

_____

_____

_____

_____

_____

_____

_____

_____

"Is that the scenario that you would like to experience?"

Copyright McGraw-Hill 2001. Original purchasers of this book are permitted to photocopy or customize this page by downloading it from www.books.mcgraw-hill.com/training/download. The document can then be opened, edited, and printed using Microsoft Word or other word processing software.

ACTIVITY SHEET 9-C
DESIRE: BUILDING THE EMOTIONAL WANT IN YOUR OFFER
(FOR A NEW PRODUCT OR SERVICE)

Choosing a new product or service you represent, complete this conversation as if you have just finished the Presentation step of the selling process, using a word picture to construct a powerful Desire statement. (*Remember that your sentence should speak to as many sensations as possible—sight, hearing, taste, touch, and smell—to stimulate the listener to live your scenario.*)

"If you were to proceed with my recommendations, here is what you will experience:

_____

_____

_____

_____

_____

_____

_____

_____

_____

_____

_____

_____

_____

_____

_____

_____

_____

_____

"Is that the scenario that you would like to experience?"

Copyright McGraw-Hill 2001. Original purchasers of this book are permitted to photocopy or customize this page by downloading it from www.books.mcgraw-hill.com/training/download. The document can then be opened, edited, and printed using Microsoft Word or other word processing software.

Objectives

1. To introduce participants to effective ways of getting commitment from prospects or customers.

2. To teach participants how to determine the potential buyer's receptivity.

3. To teach participants effective ways to ask for the business and get the order.

Time Required

15–20 minutes

Materials Needed

- One copy of each of the three activity sheets for each participant

- A flip chart or whiteboard

Mini-Seminar 10

Close: Getting the Commitment and the Order

Directions for the Trainer

1. Read the lecturette prior to your training session, and take notes so you can use it as the basis for your own comments to the group.

2. Start the training session by summarizing the lecturette in your own words for the group; then pass out the activity sheets.

3. Activity Sheet 10-A: Have participants write Trial Close questions that serve as *opinion-seeking questions* in the Close step of the selling process. Debrief by asking some of the participants to share examples with the group.

4. Activity Sheet 10-B: Have individuals develop Order Close questions that serve to *solicit a commitment* in the Close step of the selling process. Debrief by asking some of the participants to share examples with the group.

5. Activity Sheet 10-C: Have individuals develop Alternate Choice questions that *provide multiple buying options* in the Close step of the selling process. Debrief by asking some of the participants to share examples with the group.

LECTURETTE

The purpose for having a sales professional on a team is to match up prospect's or customer's needs with what an organization can provide. In making that match and building that relationship, the transaction generates a revenue stream from which people are compensated, products or services are made a reality, and growth occurs.

The salesperson who can work through the first four steps of the selling process but fails to get the business is more of a professional visitor than a professional salesperson.

The purpose of the Closing step of the selling process is to get final agreement from the potential buyer. In arriving at this point in the sales process, the professional salesperson must realize that of the myriad of closing techniques and options, there are three basic approaches to closing the sales process: a Trial Close, an Order Close, or an Alternate Choice Close.

> A *Trial Close* is used to solicit feedback from the buyer after you have made your Presentation. In a Trial Close, you are *seeking an opinion* on your offer, not soliciting a commitment.

This technique is best used when you feel the potential buyer is receptive to your offer, but you are not sure what the level of buying interest is (low, medium, or high). If you believe that the prospect or customer may not be ready to finalize the offer and purchase, then a Trial Close is a great conversation tool.

> A *Trial Close* might sound like this: "If you were to move ahead with this offer, would you want to take it with you or have it delivered?"

A Trial Close question seeks to gain an opinion from the prospect or customer in relation to the Presentation the sales professional has made and the customer's Desire to proceed with the offer. If the response appears favorable, move directly to a Close-Order Question. If the response is lukewarm or cold, then you may need to move back to step two in the sales process, Interest, and ask more questions about the customer's needs.

After a favorable conversation with a customer, at step five you may choose to simply ask for the business, or Close. A Close-Order question is one that asks for a commitment from the buyer you have been courting through the Interest, Presentation, and Desire phases. The downside to this approach is that if you have misread the customer, the response may be a resounding "No." This is very challenging to overcome. (In Mini-Seminar 15, we address how to proceed when you hear "no.")

An Order Question is a powerful Close strategy and is designed to obtain an action-oriented commitment from the prospect or customer.

A Close-Order Question might sound like this:

> "How would you like me to process your order?"

> Or, "Do you want to take this with you today?"

> Or, "How many would you like to have me order for you?"

Each of these examples assumes that the prospect or customer wants to buy and requests a commitment from the listener.

Another way of closing the selling process and seeking an order from the prospect or customer is by offering Alternate Choice options as a Close strategy. The approach is to give the prospect or customer multiple buying options.

An Alternate Choice Close might sound like this:

"Do you want this in red or green?"

Or, "Would you like a single unit or a case?"

Or, "Do you want this charged on a credit card or would you rather be billed?"

Remember these three easy, direct, and nonthreatening ways to Close the sales process with a prospect or customer and get the business.

ACTIVITY SHEET 10-A
CLOSE: GETTING THE COMMITMENT
AND THE ORDER USING TRIAL CLOSES

Develop a series of Trial Close questions for a product or service you represent. Pick your two best-selling products or services and two of your more difficult products or services. Share your completed responses with your colleagues for feedback:

Remember: A Trial Close question seeks an opinion.

1. Favorite Product or Service: _____

Trial Close Question: _____

_____

_____

_____

2. Favorite Product or Service: _____

Trial Close Question: _____

_____

_____

_____

3. Challenge Product or Service: _____

Trial Close Question: _____

_____

_____

_____

4. Challenge Product or Service: _____

Trial Close Question: _____

_____

_____

_____

Copyright McGraw-Hill 2001. Original purchasers of this book are permitted to photocopy or customize this page by downloading it from www.books.mcgraw-hill.com/training/download. The document can then be opened, edited, and printed using Microsoft Word or other word processing software.

ACTIVITY SHEET 10-B
CLOSE: GETTING THE COMMITMENT
AND THE ORDER USING CLOSE-ORDER QUESTIONS

Develop a series of Close-Order questions for a product or service you represent. Pick your two best-selling products or services and two of your more difficult products or services. Share your completed responses with your colleagues for feedback:

Remember: A Close-Order question seeks a commitment.

1. Favorite Product or Service: _____

Close-Order Question: _____

_____

_____

_____

2. Favorite Product or Service: _____

Close-Order Question: _____

_____

_____

_____

3. Challenge Product or Service: _____

Close-Order Question: _____

_____

_____

_____

4. Challenge Product or Service: _____

Close-Order Question: _____

_____

_____

_____

Copyright McGraw-Hill 2001. Original purchasers of this book are permitted to photocopy or customize this page by downloading it from www.books.mcgraw-hill.com/training/download. The document can then be opened, edited, and printed using Microsoft Word or other word processing software.

ACTIVITY SHEET 10-C
CLOSE: GETTING THE COMMITMENT
AND THE ORDER USING ALTERNATE CHOICE CLOSE

Develop a series of Alternate Choice Closing questions for a product or service you represent. Pick your two best-selling products or services and two of your more difficult products or services. Share your completed responses with your colleagues for feedback:

Remember: An Alternate Choice Close question seeks to provide options.

1. Favorite Product or Service: _____

Alternate Choice Close Question: _____

_____

_____

_____

2. Favorite Product or Service: _____

Alternate Choice Close Question: _____

_____

_____

_____

3. Challenge Product or Service: _____

Alternate Choice Close Question: _____

_____

_____

_____

4. Challenge Product or Service: _____

Alternate Choice Close Question: _____

_____

_____

_____

Copyright McGraw-Hill 2001. Original purchasers of this book are permitted to photocopy or customize this page by downloading it from www.books.mcgraw-hill.com/training/download. The document can then be opened, edited, and printed using Microsoft Word or other word processing software.

Objectives

1. To enhance participants' ability to engage in a constructive dialogue with every prospect or customer.

2. To provide participants with a systematic way in which to facilitate a dialogue, remain in control of the dialogue, increase their listening ratio, and maintain mental focus through chronological questioning.

Time Required

20–30 minutes

Materials Needed

- One copy of the activity sheet for each participant

- Transparency Master 11-A

- A flip chart or whiteboard and an overhead projector

Mini-Seminar 11

Building Relationships with the Stacking-N-Linking Conversational Model

Directions for the Trainer

1. Read the lecturette prior to your training session, and take notes so you can use it as the basis for your own comments to the group.

2. Start the training session by summarizing the lecturette in your own words for the group; then pass out the activity sheet.

3. Activity Sheet 11-A: Have participants develop a series of open-ended questions that would enhance the Interest step in the selling process by allowing a conversational selling sequence to develop. Debrief by asking some participants to share examples with the group.

4. Alternate: Activity Sheet 11-A: Have individuals or small teams develop a series of open-ended Stack-N-Link questions that could be used with a new prospect or customer to your organization. Debrief by asking the whole group what they liked and disliked about using the model. Notice the types of questions that come out of the sequence of images.

LECTURETTE

The ultimate aim of the selling process is to make prospects or customers feel comfortable with the sales professional, to the point of relaxing and engaging in a fluid conversation. The more comfortable the sales professional and the intended buyer feel with one another, open up to one another, and share with one another, the better the relationship that can develop. It is at this level that the selling process takes on a life of its own.

Some sales professionals believe that they can achieve this level of relationship by memorizing a series of questions, while others attempt to memorize specific sayings. Of course, this is not true; every selling situation is not the same, and standard questions are not always appropriate.

However, there are types of questions that need to be asked in every selling situation, as there are types of information that every salesperson must gather from the customer. It is from this valuable information that effective Presentations can be developed. All sales professionals have to be aware of these key informational targets.

An explosive technique for remembering types of core information that should be solicited and that will allow for a free flow of natural questions is referred to as Stacking-N-Linking.

You can achieve greater sales effectiveness and increased ease of dialogue with anyone if you adopt this simple conversational model. The technique focuses on two objectives:

1. *Create a mental Stack of images* that is simple to remember, perhaps even silly in nature, and sequence them from bottom to top. In essence, you will choose a series of images that you can mentally Stack one on top of another, from the floor to the ceiling. The images you select are not completely arbitrary; each will serve a valuable purpose in the questioning (Interviewing) step of the selling process.

2. *Next, take each image that you have chosen and placed into this visual stack and Link it to a purpose or questioning objective.* The power of this technique is that it is not a robotic process of asking rehearsed questions that have been memorized. Sales professionals who have been taught this technique can facilitate controlled, comfortable conversations with any prospect or customer by mentally reflecting upon the Stacked items or images, and then simply asking themselves what relational question is appropriate for the given situation.

Here is an example Stack-N-Link selling sequence that allows the sales professional to guide the conversation merely by asking strategic questions. This Stack-N-Link allows you to quickly and easily find out about the prospect, his needs and challenges, and allows you to present a solution and increase the prospect's level of Desire for your offer such that making a Close is easy.

[Display Transparency Master 11-A on the overhead projector as you describe each image from top to bottom.]

Dollar Bill Images

A Shovel

A Mean Dog Sitting in a Rocking Chair

A Series of Letter YYYYYYYYYYs

A Large Letter P Next to a ? Next to a Large Letter I

A Large Ball with Three Price Tags Hanging Off It, Going through a Goal Post

A Large, Frowning Face Resting between Crossed Swords

A Large, Double-Scoop Ice-Cream Cone

A Long Cigar

An Office Desk

A Large Nameplate

Can you recognize which series of images relates to questions that help you get to know the prospect?

Which images relate to identifying the potential problems the prospect has that you may be able to solve as a sales professional?

Finally, which images relate to the Presentation step of the selling process, presenting solutions to the customer's discovered needs?

Note that each image has a specific objective, yet that image may stimulate different questions from different sales professionals. And that is the purpose of the Stacking-N-Linking model—to make selling conversational.

[Sales trainers or sales managers may want to develop their own Stack-N-Link models that are more relevant for their organizations and teams. Reproduce the model as a wallet reminder card for your sales professionals to carry as a self-management tool. (A sample Stack-N-Link wallet card is located in the back of this book for your convenience.)]

Now let's take the Stack model and Link each image to your intended questions.

Stack-N-Link Selling Process Questions

Dollar Bill Images = The payoff for having asked good questions and listened intently, resulting in a successful transaction.

A Shovel = If any issues remain unclear, then dig (ask more questions).

A Mean Dog Sitting in = Your question, "What would it mean to you to have that challenge solved?"

A Rocking Chair = The objective is to get the prospect or customer to relax and open up.

A Series of Letter YYYYYYYYYYs = The Ys remind you to ask, "Why do you say that?" as a follow-up to the response given at the previous level.

A Large Letter P Next to a ? Next to a Large Letter I = The P represents the word Primarily and the I represents Interested in, and the question mark guides the sales professional to ask, "In looking at [insert product proposal], would you primarily be interested in . . .?"

A Large Ball with Three Price Tags Hanging Off It, Going through a Goal Post = The ball represents a single product or service you offer that best matches up to identified needs at this point. The three tags represent three associated features of that product or service that you perceive the customer might be interested in.

A Large, Frowning Face Resting between = "What are your frustrations . . .?"

Crossed Swords = "What are some of the challenges . . .?"

A Large, Double-Scoop Ice-Cream Cone = "What do you like most about your job . . .?"

A Long Cigar = "How long have you been in this position, had these responsibilities . . .?"

An Office Desk = Be certain to find out the customer's title, position, authority level, job responsibilities, and so on.

A Large Nameplate = First, get the customer's name.

Successful sales professionals make the selling process a professional act with a starting point, a middle, and a conclusion. The engagement with prospects and customers becomes a special opportunity and a valued experience. The better the conversations, the better the bonds, and the better the relationship. That adds up to better account development and more sales.

Stack-N-Link yourself to conversational selling success!

Copyright McGraw-Hill 2001. Original purchasers of this book are permitted to photocopy or customize this page by downloading it from www.books.mcgraw-hill.com/training/download. The document can then be opened, edited, and printed using Microsoft Word or other word processing software.

ACTIVITY SHEET 11-A
BUILDING RELATIONSHIPS WITH THE STACKING-N-LINKING
CONVERSATIONAL MODEL

PARTICIPANT'S
HANDOUT

Develop a series of engaging questions, working from the bottom image upward in the stacking model, that allows for a conversational approach to building Interest with a prospect or customer, ending with a sales Presentation. Share your responses with your colleagues for feedback:

Stack-N-Link Selling Sequence Questions for a New Prospect or Customer

Dollar Bill Images _____

_____

A Shovel _____

_____

A Mean Dog Sitting in a Rocking Chair _____

_____

A Series of Letter YYYYYYYYYYYs _____

_____

A Large Letter P Next to a ? Next to a Large Letter I _____

_____

A Large Ball with Three Price Tags Hanging Off It, Going through a Goal Post _____

_____

_____

A Large, Frowning Face Resting between Crossed Swords _____

_____

_____

A Large, Double-Scoop Ice-Cream Cone _____

_____

A Long Cigar _____

_____

An Office Desk _____

_____

A Large Nameplate _____

_____

_____

Copyright McGraw-Hill 2001. Original purchasers of this book are permitted to photocopy or customize this page by downloading it from www.books.mcgraw-hill.com/training/download. The document can then be opened, edited, and printed using Microsoft Word or other word processing software.

SECTION TWO
Increasing Your Team's Selling Effectiveness

Objective

1. To have participants fine-tune their selling approach, given the content of the first eleven mini-seminars.

Time Required

20–30 minutes

Materials Needed

- One copy of the activity sheet for each participant

- A list of all the products or services your organization or department offers

- A flip chart or whiteboard

- Participants' notes from previous mini-seminars

Fine-Tuning Your Sales Presentation with the Five Enhanced Selling Steps

Directions for the Trainer

1. Read the lecturette prior to your training session, and take notes so you can use it as the basis for your own comments to the group.

2. Start the training session by summarizing the lecturette in your own words for the group; then pass out the activity sheet.

3. Activity Sheet 12-A: This should be fun time with the sales professionals on your team. Review the Five Steps to Selling and the Stacking-N-Linking model presented in the first eleven mini-seminars. Then, with copies of your product or service overview sheets, have each participant role-play a favorite step of the five selling steps.

4. Activity 12-B: A selling review game:

   First, before the session, take a stack of business cards from every sales professional who will be in the session. For each sales professional, label the reverse side of several cards with a product or service your organization offers.

Second, shuffle the deck of cards and pass them around the room, having each participant take one card at a time. Let the deck go around the room several times, until all cards are drawn.

Third, using the Five Steps to Selling and focusing on the third step (the Presentation step; see Mini-Seminar 8), have a sales professional at random call out the name on a business card and the labeled item on the reverse side. That sales professional starts the selling process, using the Claim + Fact or Feature + Benefit + Naildown formula, to sell the named item.

Fourth, when the first sales professional finishes, he calls out the name on one of the business cards he is holding and the item labeled on it. That next sales professional continues the rapid-fire series by communicating how the new item can be associated (up-sold) with the previous item and why it might be a better purchase for the customer.

Have each person participate in at least one round before you debrief. Make this a fun and engaging conversational activity. Some sales professionals may have to stretch to make a connection between the previous sales professional's Presentation and theirs, and that is all right!

LECTURETTE

Practice doesn't make for perfection. Perfect practice makes for perfection. Sales professionals can easily fall victim to their own bad habits.

Develop the habit of perfect practice by revisiting the Five Steps to Selling presented in Mini-Seminars 3 through 10 and the Stacking-N-Linking conversational model presented in Mini-Seminar 11.

Sales perfection comes from perfect practice, perfect coaching, and perfect reinforcement. Sales trainers and sales managers serve as the reinforcement mechanism that allows for perfection to shine through with perfect results.

Use this mini-seminar as a follow-up and constructive review session for any material that needs reinforcement, or for a general overview of all sessions.

ACTIVITY SHEET 12-A
FINE-TUNING YOUR SALES PRESENTATION
WITH THE FIVE ENHANCED SELLING STEPS

Perfecting sales excellence is every sales professional's goal. The Five Steps to Selling and the Stacking-N-Linking conversational model can help you to attain that goal. Pair off with a colleague and coach each other as you revisit all of the work accomplished thus far (the first 11 mini-seminars) and demonstrate perfect practice of the five selling steps.

Pick your favorite product or service and a client to present to; then demonstrate your ability to flow conversationally through the selling process.

Product: _____

Prospect or Customer: _____

Five Steps of the Selling Process

    Step One: Attention Step

    Step Two: Inquiry or Interest or Needs Analysis Step

    Step Three: Presentation Step

    Step Four: Desire or Want Step

    Step Five: Close or Order Step

Attention: If there were a way to _____, would that be of interest to you? The reason that I mention this is _____.
Perhaps we can do the same for you. Would that be of interest to you?

Interest or Inquiry or Needs Analysis: In order to maximize time, may I ask you a few questions? Thank you, _____ **(Stack-N-Link)** _____.

Presentation: Based upon what we have just discussed, what would it mean to you to be able to _____?

The reason I ask is that _____

_____

_____

_____.

Desire or Want: That is the type of picture that you would like to see yourself in, isn't it?

Close or Order: Do you want to go with _____ or _____?

Copyright McGraw-Hill 2001. Original purchasers of this book are permitted to photocopy or customize this page by downloading it from www.books.mcgraw-hill.com/training/download. The document can then be opened, edited, and printed using Microsoft Word or other word processing software.

Mini-Seminar 13

Overcoming the Sales Blahs and Negative Stereotypes

Objective

1. To provide sales professionals with tools for staying energized and motivated and projecting a positive professional image.

Time Required

15–20 minutes

Materials Needed

- One copy of the activity sheet for each participant

- A flip chart or whiteboard

Directions for the Trainer

1. Read the lecturette prior to your training session and take notes so you can use it as the basis for your own comments to the group.

2. Start the training session by summarizing the lecturette in your own words for the group; then pass out the activity sheet.

3. Activity Sheet 13-A: Have participants identify three things that can zap their positive energies each day. Then have them pair off and brainstorm ways to avoid, neutralize, or convert those zappers into positives!

   Then ask participants to identify a Top Ten List of things to do to remain positive and dispel negative stereotypes. Take the combined list of actions that the sales professionals come up with and have it enlarged on a duplicating machine. Post the enlarged list on the wall for your sales team to see, refer to, and live!

   Bonus: Give participants a homework assignment of finding something, creating something, or buying something to bring to the next session that will be a symbol or reminder of a technique to use in times of despair.

LECTURETTE

Maintaining a positive appearance and positive mind-set as a sales professional is critical for sustained success. Negative situations and negative people may be daily realities in the life of a sales professional, but how one handles them can make the difference between polished professionalism and self-destruction.

Understand and embrace two keys that will differentiate you from the stereotypical negative salesperson:

First, manage your environment for maximum productivity and positive results each day!

Second, treat sales as a profession and continually commit to professional development activities!

Just as an accountant maintains a mark of professionalism as a CPA by attending classes, reading literature in that field, and participating in self-development endeavors to distinguish herself from others as a professional, so too should a professional salesperson.

A sales professional should be able to identify the activities you participate in on a regular basis to distinguish yourself from just another salesperson—taking classes, going to workshops, attending seminars, reading books, and listening to audio tapes and CDs for skill development. Your sales trainer or sales manager's job is to create an environment that is conducive to pursuing excellence.

Build your daily work schedule to include activities at the beginning and end of the day that ensure success and a positive mind-set (psychology). Recognize that the people you associate with at work and at home have a dramatic influence on who you are, the message you project to others, and thus how you are perceived overall.

> Birds of a feather flock together. Examine what your flock looks like, where they are headed, and determine whether in fact that is a flock you want to be associated with. If it's not, make a course correction today to ensure that you land at the destination you desire!

ACTIVITY SHEET 13-A
OVERCOMING THE SALES BLAHS AND
NEGATIVE STEREOTYPES

Perfecting sales excellence is every sales professional's responsibility. Developing habits, skills, traits, characteristics, tricks, and secrets for dealing with those positive-energy zappers is essential to sustained success.

Build a force field to push negatives and selling blahs away and to energize yourself. Start by identifying three things that are routine energy zappers in your job or environment; then, with a teammate, develop a list of as many positive responses to each as you can.

Positive Energy Zapper   Positive Reinforcement Action

1._____   _____
                              _____
                              _____
                              _____
                              _____
2._____   _____
                              _____
                              _____
                              _____
                              _____
3._____   _____
                              _____
                              _____
                              _____

Top Ten Things to Do Every Day to Remain Positive and Professional

1._____

2._____

3._____

4._____

5._____

6._____

7._____

8._____

9._____

10._____

Copyright McGraw-Hill 2001. Original purchasers of this book are permitted to photocopy or customize this page by downloading it from www.books.mcgraw-hill.com/training/download. The document can then be opened, edited, and printed using Microsoft Word or other word processing software.

Objectives

1. To show participants how the sales process works from an activity standpoint, so they realize that for a sale to happen, significant pre-activity must take place.

2. To show participants how each level of activity supports the next and how ample prospecting feeds into contacting, which feeds into Presentations, which feeds into Interest, and ultimately into a sale.

Time Required

15–20 minutes

Materials Needed

- One copy of each of the two activity sheets for each participant

- A flip chart or whiteboard

Directions for the Trainer

1. Read the lecturette prior to your training session, and take notes so you can use it as the basis for your own comments to the group.

2. Start the training session by passing out the activity sheets. Take a few minutes to deliver the lecturette in your own words.

3. Activity Sheet 14-A: Discuss what levels of activity presently take place at each level (prior to this mini-seminar), and then have participants identify what percentage of their overall time is spent at each of the three levels. Also, have them identify what percentage of their time is spent on each level during the actual prime selling hours for your organization (when the sales professional should be face-to-face with a prospect, engaging in the Inquiry or Interest step to identify needs or Presenting solutions that meet those needs).

Mini-Seminar 14

Using the Sales Funnel©
to Stay Sales Healthy

4. Activity Sheet 14-B: Discuss what additional activities can be undertaken at each of the three levels to increase their proficiency and success. Identify what would be a better percentage of their time to be spending at each level.

LECTURETTE

Building a solid base from which to be consistently contacting prospects and working sales or closes starts with understanding that the selling process is like a funnel. In order for a sale to come out of the bottom, there must be ample qualified prospects in the funnel to be contacted. In order for there to be qualified prospects inside the funnel, "leads" and qualified suspects must be contacted and directed into that funnel of activity.

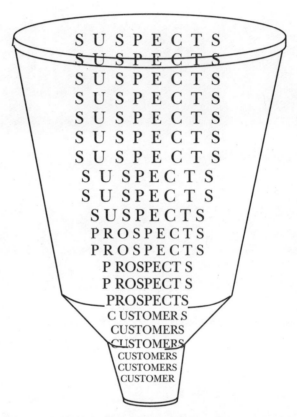

The downfall of most sales professionals is that they don't maintain consistent activity at all three levels within the Sales Funnel. Instead, many sales professionals spend a lot of time at one level, and then end up rushing and waiting. You must spend time each day, each week, and each month on all three levels equally—if one expects to make sales calls to prospects, then there must be qualified people who have previously been identified as suspects and placed into the funnel to contact.

Evaluate your present customer base to determine how many prospects had to be contacted for you to realize one sale. How many contacts with any given customer did it take to finally close the order? Next, identify how many suspect contacts it took to get that one prospect into the funnel before you could convert the prospect into a customer. The point of the funnel image is to help you recognize how many suspects it takes for you to contact to qualify a number of prospects, and how many prospect contacts it takes to successfully close one sale.

Successful sales professionals invest ample time on a regular basis to feed the funnel, work the funnel, and take care of the customers who come out the bottom.

Now let's discuss how you presently find your contacts for each level. Successful sales professionals recognize that the ability to Close a sale depends on the quality of the prospects they contact; and the quality of those prospects depends on the quality of the suspects they can identify and market the offer to.

ACTIVITY SHEET 14-A
USING THE SALES FUNNEL© TO STAY SALES HEALTHY

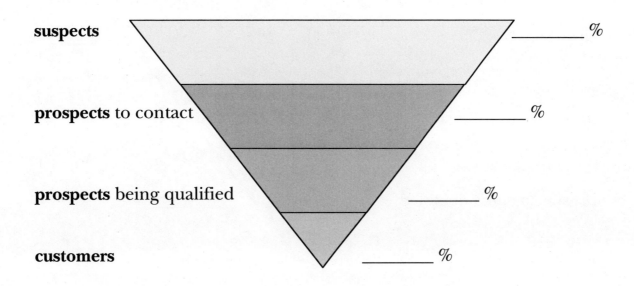

suspects _____ %

prospects to contact _____ %

prospects being qualified _____ %

customers _____ %

1. List the activities that you presently engage in at each level of the Funnel to develop Customers.

   Suspect Gathering Areas: _____

   _____

   _____

   _____

   _____

   _____

   _____

   Prospecting Activities: _____

   _____

   _____

   _____

   _____

2. Identify how much time you invested each day, prior to this mini-seminar, in each category of the Sales Funnel, if at the end of the day, all categories were to add up to 100 percent.

Copyright McGraw-Hill 2001. Original purchasers of this book are permitted to photocopy or customize this page by downloading it from www.books.mcgraw-hill.com/training/download. The document can then be opened, edited, and printed using Microsoft Word or other word processing software.

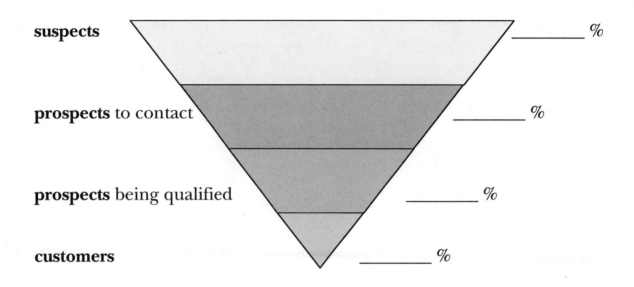

suspects _____ %

prospects to contact _____ %

prospects being qualified _____ %

customers _____ %

1. List the additional activities that you can start doing at each level of the Funnel to develop more Customers.

   Additional Suspect Gathering Activities: _____

   _____

   _____

   _____

   _____

   _____

   _____

2. Identify how much time you should invest each day in each category of the Sales Funnel now, so at the end of the day, all categories will add up to 100 percent.

Copyright McGraw-Hill 2001. Original purchasers of this book are permitted to photocopy or customize this page by downloading it from www.books.mcgraw-hill.com/training/download. The document can then be opened, edited, and printed using Microsoft Word or other word processing software.

Objectives

1. To help participants become more proficient at identifying better prospects to invest their time in, by understanding the characteristics of a viable customer.

2. To have participants develop a profile of an ideal new customer, to guide all selling activities.

3. To help participants recognize where their personal business comes from and what percentage of their business comes from actual selling time.

Time Required

15–20 minutes

Materials Needed

- One copy of each of the two activity sheets for each participant

- A flip chart or whiteboard

Directions for the Trainer

1. Read the lecturette prior to your training session, and take notes so you can use it as the basis for your own comments to the group.

2. Start the training session by passing out the activity sheets. Take a few minutes to deliver the lecturette in your own words.

3. Activity Sheet 15-A: Have participants describe their ideal customers from their experience. Have them list the characteristics of a qualified customer from their present client lists. Then have each participant partner with a colleague to determine the similarities and differences in their lists.

4. Activity Sheet 15-B: Have participants refine their lists to develop a more specific profile for the ideal Prospect and a profile for the Prospect Organization.

Mini-Seminar 15

Qualifying Your Profile Customer and Understanding the 80/20 Rule

LECTURETTE

Many sales professionals work hard every day pursuing every contact that comes their way, never realizing that while there may appear to be a lot of activity, there is little real productivity. One way to focus the activity so that it equals productivity is to study the quality of your present customers.

Analyze your present customers to determine whether a large percentage of your business is coming from certain types of customers. Most sales professionals will recognize a trend, which is referred to as a Profile. Once you recognize that you tend to connect with certain types of prospects better than others and that more of your business comes from these specific types of prospects, you can focus your immediate energies each day to ensure that those prospects are being connected with.

An Italian landowner and economist, Pareto, recognized one day as he took inventory of the Italian countryside that 80 percent of the land and wealth was held by 20 percent of the people. Commonly referred to as the 80/20 rule, his theory often holds true in sales that 80 percent of our business comes from 20 percent of our clients. Unfortunately, the reverse is also true of many unsuccessful sales professionals: They spend up to 80 percent of their time with those customers who constitute only 20 percent of the business.

Sales professionals need to recognize the characteristics of their core customer base: Who are they, where are they, and how many more of them are not being contacted?

Examine your present customer base and analyze the patterns and trends among your customers to determine whether there are common ingredients among a pool of customers. If so, develop the commonalities into a Profile that can serve as a map for finding more customers like them.

Developing a customer Profile is a critical turning point in sustained, successful selling; all your future marketing, advertising, promotional, and selling efforts can be fine-tuned to speak first to those people who match the Profile—potential customers for your organization's products or services.

ACTIVITY SHEET 15-A
QUALIFYING YOUR PROFILE CUSTOMER
AND UNDERSTANDING THE 80/20 RULE

Describe the present typical customer contact on your active client or customer list. Most often they tend to be:

Age Range: _____

Gender: _____

Ethnicity: _____

How long have they been with organizations they represent? _____

How long have they been in the industry they represent? _____

How long have they been customers of your organization? _____

How long have you been working with them? _____

What geographical region are they in? _____

What dollar figure of business do they represent to you? _____

How many items of business do they represent for you?_____

Other: _____

_____

_____

_____

_____

_____

_____

_____

_____

_____

_____

_____

_____

_____

_____

_____

_____

Copyright McGraw-Hill 2001. Original purchasers of this book are permitted to photocopy or customize this page by downloading it from www.books.mcgraw-hill.com/training/download. The document can then be opened, edited, and printed using Microsoft Word or other word processing software.

ACTIVITY SHEET 15-B
QUALIFYING YOUR PROFILE CUSTOMER
AND UNDERSTANDING THE 80/20 RULE

Personal: Now describe what the present personal customer contact on your active client or customer list should look like:

Age Range: _____

Gender: _____

Ethnicity: _____

How long have they been with organizations they represent? _____

How long have they been in the industry they represent? _____

How long have they been customers of your organization? _____

How long have you been working with them? _____

What geographical region are they in? _____

What dollar figure of business do they represent to you? _____

How many items of business do they represent for you?_____

Other: _____

_____

_____

_____

Organizational: Now describe what the present organizational customer contact on your active client or customer list should look like:

Industry: _____

Size in Revenue: _____

Number of Employees:_____

How long have they been in the industry they represent? _____

How long have they been a customer of your organization? _____

How long have you been working with them? _____

What geographical region are they in? _____

What dollar figure of business do they represent to you? _____

How many items of business do they represent for me? _____

Other: _____

_____

_____

_____

Copyright McGraw-Hill 2001. Original purchasers of this book are permitted to photocopy or customize this page by downloading it from www.books.mcgraw-hill.com/training/download. The document can then be opened, edited, and printed using Microsoft Word or other word processing software.

Objectives

1. To help participants recognize that better qualifying of suspect pools and better quality suspects result in an improved sales process, shortened sales Presentation cycles, and increased sales closes.

2. To have participants develop a clear Profile of a Qualified Suspect based upon quantifiable descriptors.

Time Required

15–20 minutes

Materials Needed

• One copy of each of the two activity sheets for each participant

• A flip chart or whiteboard

Directions for the Trainer

1. Read the lecturette prior to your training session, and take notes so you can use it as the basis for your own comments to the group.

2. Start the training session by passing out the activity sheets. Take a few minutes to deliver the lecturette in your own words.

3. Activity Sheet 16-A: Have participants identify all the characteristics of a qualified contact who they would presently call a Qualified Suspect. Debrief by pointing out similarities and differences among sales professionals, especially noting the differences if the sales professionals are all selling the same product or service!

4. Activity Sheet 16-B: Have each participant pair off with a colleague to develop a more comprehensive description and more precise Qualified Suspect Profile to guide their pre-selling and qualifying efforts.

Mini-Seminar 16

Designing a Qualified Suspect Profile for Increased Sales

LECTURETTE

Great sales professionals never run out of qualified prospects. That is in part due to the fact that they are consistently putting their names out in areas where they know there are Qualified Suspects.

Examine how you prospect for leads and where you tend to get leads from. Remember that **a Qualified Prospect is someone who, at a minimum:**

> **First, has a need for what you offer;**
>
> **Second, has the capacity to buy; and**
>
> **Third, has an urgency to buy now!**

With this formula in mind, the sales professional's job is to ask two questions:

1. "Which of my leads would I call Suspects?"

2. "How would I describe this lead if I were attempting to develop a Qualified Suspect Profile for contacting?"

Recognize that it is easy to fall into the trap of waiting for the leads or contacts to come to you. Not many Suspects will do this. It is also easy to become complacent if you appear to have a volume of Suspects. Remember that it takes time to find these Suspects and get them into the Sales Funnel, and more time to work the Prospects in the Funnel to get a Customer to fall out the bottom. If you have no new leads or Suspects to work because you have been spending all your time in the middle or bottom of the Funnel, now is the time to find and contact new Suspects. Realize the need to work evenly and consistently at all three levels of the Funnel. In the final analysis, the sale can't take place if you are not continually feeding the Funnel with Qualified Suspects!

Successful sales professionals can't be all things to all people, so you must understand what the characteristics are of the ideal candidate who you connect with best and personally tend to convert to the most sales. This well-defined Qualified Suspect Profile then will guide all your future actions (marketing, networking, promotions, advertising, etc.).

It's important to recognize exactly what a Qualified Suspect looks like and to develop a Profile of that Suspect. This will assist in identifying a potential Suspect to engage in the Five Steps to Selling. It will also help you avoid spending too much time on an unqualified Suspect who might waste both of your time.

With a clearer understanding of your targeted Qualified Suspect Profile in mind, you can examine the contacts you make to determine the level of engagement that is appropriate. As you examine how much time is invested in building the contact relationships forged at the Suspect level, the time required at the Prospect level, and the time required at the Customer level, you will be better able to channel your efforts accordingly.

Most sales professionals invest a majority of their energies in the most contact-rich environments. Studies done in the late 1990's by Frank Ruck and Jeff Magee determined that most customers come from only 10 percent of available market options.

View Suspects for your offer as aligning into a sales curve, called the Ruck-Magee Customer Curve, which indicates that about 10 percent of the Suspect pool can easily be turned into Customers. About another 10 percent of Suspects will never become Customers. The remaining 80 percent represent potential Customers available from the middle Suspect pool.

First, spend time prospecting with the 10 percent of Suspects who are most likely to become Customers.. Then invest time where most sales professionals forget to work, in the large middle of the Suspect pool, where 80 percent of your potential Customers are. Finally, don't waste time with the 10 percent of Suspects who will never buy your offer.

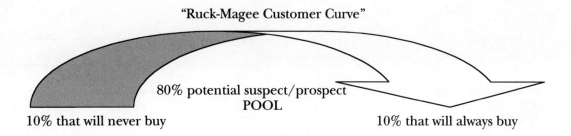

"Ruck-Magee Customer Curve"

80% potential suspect/prospect
POOL

10% that will never buy   10% that will always buy

With a Qualified Suspect Profile in mind, you will be better able to recognize a contact in the middle of the curve who best matches a solution you can offer. The bottom line will be increased contact effectiveness, reduced missed contacts, and increased sales.

ACTIVITY SHEET 16-A
DESIGNING A QUALIFIED SUSPECT PROFILE FOR INCREASED
SALES INDIVIDUAL EXERCISE

List the characteristics and traits of a present Suspect who you would attempt to engage in the selling process.

_____

_____

_____

_____

_____

_____

_____

_____

_____

_____

_____

_____

_____

_____

_____

_____

_____

_____

Copyright McGraw-Hill 2001. Original purchasers of this book are permitted to photocopy or customize this page by downloading it from www.books.mcgraw-hill.com/training/download. The document can then be opened, edited, and printed using Microsoft Word or other word processing software.

ACTIVITY SHEET 16-B
DESIGNING A QUALIFIED SUSPECT PROFILE FOR INCREASED
SALES TEAM EXERCISE

List the characteristics and traits of a future Suspect who you could engage in the selling process.

_____

_____

_____

_____

_____

_____

_____

_____

_____

_____

_____

_____

_____

_____

_____

_____

_____

_____

_____

Copyright McGraw-Hill 2001. Original purchasers of this book are permitted to photocopy or customize this page by downloading it from www.books.mcgraw-hill.com/training/download. The document can then be opened, edited, and printed using Microsoft Word or other word processing software.

Objectives

1. To help participants better understand what "No" means and doesn't mean.

2. To have participants develop action plans for what to do when they encounter "no."

Time Required

15–20 minutes

Materials Needed

* One copy of the activity sheet for each participant

* A flip chart or whiteboard

Directions for the Trainer

1. Read the lecturette prior to your training session, and take notes so you can use it as the basis for your own comments to the group.

2. Start the training session by passing out the activity sheets. Take a few minutes to deliver the lecturette in your own words.

3. Activity Sheet 17-A: Have participants develop a series of conversational responses that can be used when they encounter "No" from a prospect.

Mini-Seminar 17

Overcoming "No"

LECTURETTE

It has been said that the greatest barrier to selling success is when the sales professional takes a "No" response from a suspect, prospect, or customer personally. All sales professionals must realize that when a buyer says "No" to them, the specific word "No" is a response to the offer as it was presented. The "No" is not a rejection of the sales professional as a person.

Every sales professional has heard varying statistics suggesting that most prospects become customers and thus the sale takes place after the *n*th rejection. *Professional Selling Power* magazine published an article about a study done by JMI, Inc., which indicated that most sales take place after at least five rejections. At what number do you typically give up on a suspect, prospect, or customer?

"No" is merely a verbal response to an offer. The art of selling really begins at the first "No." The questions a sales professional must begin asking at that moment are:

1. Does "No" mean, "Not right now" (timing issues)?

2. Does "No" mean, "I don't have the money to buy right now" (revenue, budget, or billing issues)?

3. Does "No" mean, "I don't have the authority" (buying power or decision-making ability)?

4. Does "No" mean, "We can't use it or don't need it right now" (inappropriate need level for that specific offer only)?

5. Does "No" mean, "I don't want to make the decision" (decision makers are changing, or your contact is leaving the organization and doesn't want to make the commit for a successor)?

Realize that until you "know" what "No" means, you shouldn't accept "No" without engaging in a dialogue to determine precisely what it means.

Knowing exactly what "No" means gives the sales professional conversational power in the selling process.

ACTIVITY SHEET 17-A
OVERCOMING "NO"

Develop a series of responses or questions that could be offered at the moment a suspect, prospect, or customer says "No." Tailor your questions for each of the situations given.

(Wrong timing) _____

_____

_____

_____ ?

(Money or revenue problems) _____

_____

_____

_____ ?

(Lack of buying power or authority) _____

_____

_____

_____ ?

(No need) _____

_____

_____

_____ ?

(Impending change in position or players) _____

_____

_____

_____ ?

Copyright McGraw-Hill 2001. Original purchasers of this book are permitted to photocopy or customize this page by downloading it from www.books.mcgraw-hill.com/training/download. The document can then be opened, edited, and printed using Microsoft Word or other word processing software.

Objectives

1. To help participants develop skills for constructively handling objections in the sales Presentation process.

2. To teach participants how to respond to an objection using the Sandwich technique.

Time Required

15–20 minutes

Materials Needed

- One copy of the activity sheet for each participant

- A plain hamburger from a fast-food restaurant (bun and meat only)

- A flip chart or whiteboard

Directions for the Trainer

1. Read the lecturette prior to your training session, and take notes so you can use it as the basis for your own comments to the group.

2. Start the training session by passing out the activity sheets. Take a few minutes to deliver the lecturette in your own words.

3. Activity Sheet 18-A: Have participants complete the activity sheets. Then ask them to pair with a colleague and role-play responding to objections heard in a typical sales Presentation, using some of the techniques you have presented. Debrief by asking some of the pairs to share examples with the whole group.

Mini-Seminar 18

Dealing with Objections for Constructive Outcomes

LECTURETTE

The fear and anxiety that come over a sales professional at the instant the prospect or customer utters an objection during the Presentation can be alarming. Prepare ahead to be aware of potential objections and to have logical effective responses at the ready.

Many times an objection is simply a question in disguise. Become adept at listening to the objection to determine if a question-in-disguise is being asked. Then you can guide the conversation in a constructive direction. The keys are to listen closely, and to respond, not react.

A great way to determine if an objection is the only obstacle to the potential sale is to ask an **Objection Qualification Question**, like this:

> "I can appreciate your concern with _____ [insert the exact objection statement] __. Let me ask you, if we could address that concern satisfactorily, would you be in a position to move ahead with this offer?"

Asking this question will help you find out whether there are other obstacles or future objections that may arise. By confirming this objection, you can single focus on addressing the precise barrier. Then the Presentation phase (the third step in the selling process) can proceed directly to the last step, asking for the order, or Close.

If the prospect or customer is reluctant to proceed, then you may want to ask:

> "Obviously, there is something else causing you to hesitate. Would you mind sharing that with me?"

This question works to draw out conversationally the hidden (and possibly the true) objection to be addressed.

If the objection turns into resistance, then the sales professional should mentally evaluate the situation and, if appropriate, ask questions to re-qualify the person according to the criteria developed in Mini-Seminar 15. Also recall the three criteria presented in Mini-Seminar 16: A Qualified Prospect is someone who, at a minimum:

First, has a need for what you offer;

Second, has the capacity to buy; and

Third, has an urgency to buy now!

A successful sales professional must address any valid objection in the conversational sales approach. Any objection left unaddressed may grow in the prospect's or customer's mind to such a level that it may cause the buyer to say "No."

Once the precise objection has been identified, it is now up to you to determine whether that objection can be addressed. If it can, then move the sales process from whatever step you were in to the third step, and present the most applicable and powerful Claim + Feature + Benefit + Naildown sequence you can. (See Mini-Seminars 3 and 8 for review.)

The Naildown question is a powerful way to put that objection to rest and move back to the point in the conversation where the objection came about.

One way to visualize how to address an objection is to use the Sandwich Technique. In this technique, you construct your response as if you were making a sandwich— To do this, respond to an objection in three steps (three statements)—nothing extra needs to be said or done:

1. Visualize the base piece of bun = Make a positive reference or statement.

2. Visualize the piece of meat = Restate the objection or negative issue.

3. Visualize the top piece of bun = Make a positive reference or statement.

[Direction to trainer: Use the sandwich you brought to this session as a visual demonstration of how to verbally respond, as if you were making a sandwich in three steps.]

As the top piece of bread is placed and a corresponding Naildown statement is given, imagine someone piercing the sandwich with a large toothpick (nail) to hold the entire technique together.

Here is an example of how the Sandwich technique might sound:

> "I can appreciate your concern with __(insert objection)__. [This sentence serves as the base bun and is an empathy statement.] That is a genuine concern. [This is the meat, the substance of the objection.] There are several ways we can address this: _____.[This is the top piece of bun, a positive response.] That does address your initial objection, doesn't it? [The last sentence is a Naildown statement.]"

ACTIVITY SHEET 18-A
DEALING WITH OBJECTIONS FOR CONSTRUCTIVE OUTCOMES

Develop a series of responses or questions that could be offered at the moment a suspect, prospect, or customer poses an objection. Then team with a colleague and role-play verbalizing what you have written.

Identify a product or service you would present: _____

Identify a Qualified Prospect Profile you would be talking with: _____

_____

_____

Identify a typical objection that you might hear: _____

_____

What sort of question would you ask now to qualify and quantify that objection? _____

_____

_____

_____

_____

_____

Assume the prospect or customer gave an affirmative response to your question. How would you address that objection in your new Presentation step? (What Feature + Benefit + Naildown sequence would you use?) _____

_____

_____

_____

_____

_____

_____

_____

_____

_____

_____

Copyright McGraw-Hill 2001. Original purchasers of this book are permitted to photocopy or customize this page by downloading it from www.books.mcgraw-hill.com/training/download. The document can then be opened, edited, and printed using Microsoft Word or other word processing software.

Objectives

1. To enhance the participants' ability to present effectively and to determine what components influence the overall purchase decision by the customer.

2. To teach participants to recognize the four specific opportunities for a Presentation to be derailed.

Time Required

15–20 minutes

Materials Needed

- One copy of the activity sheet for each participant

- A flip chart or whiteboard

The Four Mental Decisions Associated with Every Purchase Transaction

Directions for the Trainer

1. Read the lecturette prior to your training session, and take notes so you can use it as the basis for your own comments to the group.

2. Start the training session by taking a few minutes to deliver the lecturette in your own words. Then pass out a deck of 3- by 5-inch index cards (or similar cards), each with one of the Four Mental Decisions written on it.

3. Activity Sheet 19-A: Have participants pair off, keeping their respective cards concealed from their partners. Participant will take turns assuming the roles of sales professional and prospect. The sales professional will role-play a sales Presentation for any product or service he chooses. The prospect or customer will hesitate to buy what is being presented, based on buying decision objection written on his card. It will be the sales professional's job to determine what the objection is by asking questions and

making observations. Allow a few minutes for each Presentation, then have the teams reverse roles. Debrief by asking the pairs to share what they learned with the group.

LECTURETTE

Whenever anyone makes a purchase, there are four different decisions that must be successfully addressed for the transaction to occur. At any one of the four decision points, an objection can arise. This process goes on whenever you are making a Presentation to a prospect or customer.

Many sales professionals become so intent on presenting the facts or features and the benefits that they may not even recognize when they have cornered themselves in their own Presentation, by not addressing a core decision factor.

Studies indicate that in every buying and selling transaction, the decision maker always makes four basic mental decisions in evaluating an offer. In some selling Presentations, multiple decision makers are involved in the process. In that case, each of the decision makers makes these four specific decisions. Focus on the four core decisions and don't become sidetracked by the number of individuals involved in the process.

The four core mental decisions considered in every buying transaction are:

1. **Financial:** Can we afford it and does it make economic sense?

2. **Technical:** Does this offer address what we really need? Does it address our technical requirements, regulations, laws, project needs, client needs, and so on?

3. **User:** Will we really use it, and will we gain enough use to justify the investment, price, or cost? Will the person this is being bought for use it, or will it be a source of conflict at home or at work?

4. **Coach:** Is the offer appealing? This is the internal voice that likes the offer and may like the sales professional and encourages you to just go for it. It may also be a person who champions the offer.

Every successful Presentation must address all four decisions respectfully. If any of the decisions are not addressed professionally but the sales transaction takes place anyway, the results can be disastrous:

1. Buyer's remorse occurs when you buy something, get home, and then realize that the purchase has caused a financial problem or burden. You realize that you are not using the product as intended; you got caught up in the emotion of the sales transaction and made a purchase that now doesn't make sense to you. You might return the item; if you keep it, you might never return to where you bought it

2. Intimidation occurs when you reflect back on what you purchased and realize it has too many gadgets, too much power in respect to what you actually needed—you were oversold. What seemed to suit you during the Presentation is now intimidating.

3. Frustration occurs when you reflect back upon what you bought, realizing that you did not really need it, nor will you really use it. Your Coach got the best of you. Now you become mad at yourself and resentful toward the sales professional and the organization he represents.

Mis-selling can create future selling challenges as well as present problems. Successful selling centers on, addresses, and does not avoid these four core mental decisions. The cornerstone of successful selling is to qualify your prospect or customers to ensure:

1. They can afford the offer!

2. The offer speaks to their specific requirements for performance!

3. They will in fact use and benefit from the offer!

4. They are really satisfied with the offer; they want it!

Successful selling addresses these four core mental decisions every time.

ACTIVITY SHEET 19-A
THE FOUR MENTAL DECISIONS ASSOCIATED
WITH EVERY PURCHASE TRANSACTION:
LEARN HOW TO IDENTIFY EACH

Pair off with a role-playing partner, keeping your card concealed.

You will each, in turn, assume the role of sales professional and prospect. The sales professional will role-play a sales Presentation for any chosen product or service. The prospect or customer will hesitate to buy what is being presented, based on the buying decision objection written on your card. It will be the sales professional's job to determine what the objection is by asking questions and making observations.

Allow a few minutes for each Presentation, then reverse roles.

Copyright McGraw-Hill 2001. Original purchasers of this book are permitted to photocopy or customize this page by downloading it from www.books.mcgraw-hill.com/training/download. The document can then be opened, edited, and printed using Microsoft Word or other word processing software.

Objective

1. To teach participants how to short-en the selling process by determin-ing early in the process the capacity of the potential buyer to buy or ac-cept the offer being made.

Time Required

15–20 minutes

Materials Needed

- One copy of the activity sheet for each participant

- A flip chart or whiteboard

Directions for the Trainer

1. Read the lecturette prior to your training session and take notes so you can use it as the basis for your own comments to the group.

2. Start the training session by passing out the activity sheets. Take a few minutes to deliver the lecturette in your own words.

3. Activity Sheet 20-A: Have partici-pants pair off to discuss each sce-nario and come up with questions that could be used conversationally to determine the prospect's capacity to accept the offer.

Mini-Seminar 20

Designing Core Dis-Qualifying Questions

LECTURETTE

The sales professional's ability to conversationally ask the hard questions is critical to sustaining sales success.

Three of the hardest types of questions for most sales professionals to ask are about:

1. financial constraints,

2. user constraints, and

3. timeline constraints.

Sales professionals do the prospect or customer a disservice by avoiding these questions. Learn to ask simple questions like:

1. "Does this proposal or offer fall within the financial parameters you were expecting?" Or, "Is there a budget range we need to be sensitive to?"

2. "Does this look like something that can be easily used to address your needs?" Or, "What do you like most about what we are talking about in respect to _____ (insert the product or service being discussed)_____?"

3. "Is there a specific date you were expecting to complete the purchase by?" Or, "Is there some urgency to getting this _____ and having it in use?"

Among the many questions that a sales professional may want to ask a prospect or customer, there are universal question targets that must be addressed. The earlier you ask these questions, the better able you will be to determine how best to meet the prospect's or customer's needs. This can help you to either move toward a close more efficiently, or determine quickly that the buyer isn't qualified and therefore terminate the dialogue.

The point of asking Dis-Qualifying Questions is that you assume every prospect can afford your offer. Ask the questions; let prospects tell you if they can't buy your offer.

ACTIVITY SHEET 20-A
DESIGNING CORE DIS-QUALIFYING QUESTIONS

Pair off with a role-playing partner and take turns working through these scenarios. One person assumes the role of buyer, the other the role of seller. Sell through the scenario presented and develop multiple conversational questions that could be used in each scenario, as well as responses to each objection.

Scenario One—Financial:

Susan is a buyer and wants to spend less than your retail price point. She has alternative sources of funding that she can access if desired. What would you do?

_____

_____

_____

_____

Scenario Two—User:

Tom is looking at your product or service but has not asked any questions about its application or utilization; his interest has been around several other buying decision concerns. You have had a dialogue with him concerning finance, time line for acquisition, and whether the product is desired. What have you not addressed and how could you address it?

_____

_____

_____

_____

Scenario Three—Timeline:

A corporate buyer is on the telephone inquiring about rushed delivery options. Your normal delivery mechanism won't meet the customer's needs. How could you proceed?

_____

_____

_____

_____

Copyright McGraw-Hill 2001. Original purchasers of this book are permitted to photocopy or customize this page by downloading it from www.books.mcgraw-hill.com/training/download. The document can then be opened, edited, and printed using Microsoft Word or other word processing software.

Objectives

1. To help participants recognize that it may be appropriate to alter their sales approach based upon the age segmentation of the buyer.

2. To show participants multiple approaches for interacting with buyers, based upon their age segmentation.

Time Required

20–30 minutes

Materials Needed

- One copy of the activity sheet for each participant

- A flip chart or whiteboard

Directions for the Trainer

1. Read the lecturette prior to your training session, and take notes so you can use it as the basis for your own comments to the group.

2. Start the training session by taking a few minutes to deliver the lecturette in your own words. Then pass out copies of the activity sheet to each participant.

3. Activity Sheet 21-A: Have participants pair off in age segmentation groupings and complete the activity sheets. Then have each team select a presenter to share a brief overview of the pair's findings with the entire group. Debrief by asking some participants to share what they learned with the group.

Mini-Seminar 21

Selling to the Five Different Age Segmentations

LECTURETTE

For the first time in recorded history, today's workplace consists of a very unique demographic trend: five distinct age segmentations all working at the same time. How each group has been raised and conditioned and how each operates varies dramatically. The ability of the sales professional to recognize this unique situation and tailor a sales approach, questions, and the overall Presentation to each particular generational segmentation will significantly impact your selling ability.

Census statistics and data charts in a recent managerial leadership text, *Coaching for Impact* (Dr. Jeffrey Magee and Dr. Jay Kent-Ferraro, Brown Book Publishing, 2000), reveal five distinct generational segmentations in today's workplace:

1. **Centurions** are workers (and thus potential buyers) over the age of 55; this group is estimated to be more than 55 million individuals.

2. **Baby boomers** are individuals between 37 and 55; this group is estimated to be more than 43 million individuals.

3. **Generation X** are individuals between 27 and 37; this group is estimated at more than 30 million individuals.

4. **Generation Y** are individuals between 20 and 27; this group is estimated at more than 26 million individuals.

5. **Generation MTV** (also known by some as the dot-com babies or the Mosaic generation) are younger than 20; this group is estimated at more than 53 million individuals.

The approach with each generational segmentation is not a matter of good versus bad or right versus wrong. How you engage each group directly correlates to how each group was raised and what matters to each group.

How you engage in a dialogue, what you might say or not say, may be within the norm for how you talk and act with your peer group. But to have the same level of effectiveness in interacting with a segmentation that is significantly older or younger than you, your approach may have to be different.

For example, studies indicate that these are some of the characteristics of each segmentation:

1. Centurions are more conservative, will scrutinize change, exhibit more loyal behavior patterns, are very patient, are more formal and structured.

2. Baby boomers are more results-oriented, power- and action-focused, and tend to be more concerned with image or reputation and materialism, are conditionally patient, relatively structured and formal in their public impressions and actions.

3. Generation Xers are fast, action-oriented individuals, like net worth options, are me-centered and not very loyal or patient, tend to resist structure or formalities, and feel everyone is their equal.

4. Generation Yers are into extreme actions, offers, differentiating themselves from the pack, are not very loyal or patient, loyalty is conditional upon their wants, are not very structured, and tend to shy away from formalities.

5. Generation MTVers are searching for meaning, want relationships, and need structure.

The success of the sales professional in engaging each segmentation is contingent upon your ability to understand these variances. Once an educated guess is made as to the specific generational segmentation of the potential buyer, and keeping in mind the generational segmentation you represent, adjust your actions and approach to be mindful of where the buyer comes from and what his values are.

ACTIVITY SHEET 21-A
SELLING TO THE FIVE DIFFERENT AGE SEGMENTATIONS

PARTICIPANT'S HANDOUT

Pair off in teams reflective of each generational segmentation and discuss how you think each person would act, react, or respond given each category and how that would influence your selling style. Then share your thoughts and impressions with your colleagues. Notice how each team, made up of a different generational segmentation, interprets each category.

	Centurion	Baby Boomer	Gen. X	Gen. Y	MTV
Loyalty					
Dedication					
Patience					
Attention					
Interest					
Formality					
Risk Levels					
Finance					
Technology					
Time					
Emotions					
Other:					

Copyright McGraw-Hill 2001. Original purchasers of this book are permitted to photocopy or customize this page by downloading it from www.books.mcgraw-hill.com/training/download. The document can then be opened, edited, and printed using Microsoft Word or other word processing software.

Objectives

1. To help participants recognize that it may be appropriate to alter their sales approach based upon the gender of the buyer.

2. To help participants learn multiple approaches for interacting with a buyer based upon gender.

Time Required

20–30 minutes

Materials Needed

- One copy of the activity sheet for each participant

- A flip chart or whiteboard

Directions for the Trainer

1. Read the lecturette prior to your training session, and take notes so you can use it as the basis for your own comments to the group.

2. Start the training session by taking a few minutes to deliver the lecturette in your own words. Then pass out copies of the activity sheet to each participant.

3. Activity Sheet 22-A: Have participants pair off into gender-specific groups and complete the activity sheets. Then have each team select a presenter to share a brief overview of their findings with the entire group. Debrief by asking some participants to share what they learned with the group.

Mini-Seminar 22

Selling to Gender-Specific Needs

LECTURETTE

Sales professionals have known for decades that the buying styles of men and women differ. The advertising world has studied, tested, and conducted focus groups; run split campaigns and different ads; and varied pricing, colors, sizes, names, smells, and so on, all in an attempt to determine what works best for men and for women. While some very definitive answers have been determined, there are still a lot of unknowns and even a larger number of similarities among men and women in a buying mode.

Sales professionals must recognize that how one engages a male versus a female prospect or customer should be different in respect to their buying behaviors, not in the level of professionalism afforded to each individual. This understanding will greatly influence how you navigate the Five Steps to the Selling Process. The gender of the prospect or customer may influence your approach in these ways:

1. Engage in Attention-getting conversations, as a component of the first selling step. Although there are exceptions, women tend to be more relationship-based than men and want to feel comfortable with the sales professional before revealing personal information, as in step two of the selling process—Inquiry or Interest. Men tend to be more aggressive and bottom-line-oriented and will answer questions more quickly. Men may also be less engaged in step one than women.

2. Men may want to be more specific in the questioning phase of the selling process, Step Two—Inquiry or Interest, whereas a women may have a wide range of differing questions or answers they want to reveal.

3. Men in the Presentation step typically want to hear about the bottom-line results the product or service will generate. They tend to want to focus on the features and benefits that are of interest to them. Although women may also want to hear about these tangibles, they may also want to hear in the Presentation step how the product or service correlates to their bigger picture responsibilities in life.

It is important for sales professionals to recognize that differing product or services have a wide range of Features and Benefits. Your Features and Benefit statements may have to be changed to reflect what might interest a female buyer as opposed to what might be more influential with a male buyer.

Remember, people buy for differing reasons. In addition to the influencers to buying decisions already discussed, another influencer is gender, like it or not!

ACTIVITY SHEET 22-A
SELLING TO GENDER-SPECIFIC NEEDS

PARTICIPANT'S HANDOUT

Pair off into two teams, one of men and a second of women, and discuss how you feel a buyer of each gender would act, react, or respond in each category and how that would influence your selling style. Then share your thoughts and impressions with your colleagues.

Caution: Notice the similarities and differences, energy, tension and potential emotions that may reveal themselves, both in your gender-specific groups and as a large group when you debrief. There are no right or wrong responses, just perspectives for consideration!

	Men	Women
Loyalty		
Dedication		
Patience		
Attention		
Interest		
Formality		
Risk Levels		
Finance		
Technology		
Time		
Emotions		
Other:		

Copyright McGraw-Hill 2001. Original purchasers of this book are permitted to photocopy or customize this page by downloading it from www.books.mcgraw-hill.com/training/download. The document can then be opened, edited, and printed using Microsoft Word or other word processing software.

Objective

1. To help participants enhance their abilities to focus on a person individually and close out all distractions.

Time Required

15–20 minutes

Materials Needed

- One copy of the activity sheet for each participant

- A flip chart or whiteboard

Directions for the Trainer

1. Read the lecturette prior to your training session, and take notes so you can use it as the basis for your own comments to the group.

2. After you deliver the lecturette, hand out copies of the activity sheet.

3. Activity Sheet 23-A: Explain that participants will have 10 minutes to meet as many people in the session as possible, find out information about others, and fill in the bingo game. Let the activity continue until most participants have completed the game. Debrief by asking participants to share how they felt about asking and answering the questions. Are there better ways to focus on another person in a one-on-one situation to find out volumes of data?

Mini-Seminar 23

Selling to Individuals in One-on-One Situations

LECTURETTE

The annals of recent sales history are full of stories of exceedingly powerful people in the sales world reaching the pinnacle of their industries by making people feel as if they were the only person on the planet.

1. Mary Kay Ash of Mary Kay Cosmetics fame is known for opening her home to her sales stars at conventions and rewarding super-achievers with pictures, handwritten notes, and of course, the well-known pink Cadillacs. Many have had the opportunity to dialogue with Mary Kay personally. They report that she shakes your hand genuinely and firmly, holds onto your hand or arm, looks you directly in the eyes, and addresses you by name. She continues looking at you for the duration of the dialogue. Never does she look beyond you to see if someone more important has entered the area, or become distracted by other activities around her.

2. Sam Walton of Wal-Mart fame is famous and successful for many reasons. One of the keys to Wal-Mart's success is that each store is staffed at the front door by an individual whose sole job is to meet and greet all arrivals and make them feel welcome, by presenting a smile, a greeting, and an offer of help.

Sales professionals must realize that any signal sent to a prospect or customer that he is not as important as someone or something else can cause the customer to tune the sales professional out.

When engaging the prospect or customer in one-on-one situations, follow these guideposts to help you to block out all potential distractions and focus on the other person:

1. Make eye contact. (Can you remember the eye color of the last person you talked with?)

2. Notice the color of the hair and the hairstyle.

3. Take vivid mental notes, or better yet, have a writing utensil and something to write on to take physical notes.

4. Call the person by name, making sure to get the correct pronunciation. If follow-up correspondence will be necessary, get the correct spelling of all names—don't assume anything.

5. Remember that the correct ratio is to listen twice as much as you talk. (You have one mouth and two ears; utilize them in that same ratio.)

6. Find something you have in common with the person (home location, hobby, schooling, vocation, industry, etc.)

Building relationships with people one person at a time can be done more effectively if you first connect with individuals one-on-one.

ACTIVITY SHEET 23-A
SELLING TO INDIVIDUALS IN ONE-ON-ONE SITUATIONS

One-on-One Bingo

Identify someone in this mini-seminar who meets the criteria written in each bingo square, and write the name of the appropriate person in each square. See how many bingo line-ups you can get before time runs out.

Same Name As You	Same Industry As You	Brown Eyes
Blonde Hair	Brown Hair	Same Vocation As You
Blue Eyes	Gray Hair	Black Hair

Copyright McGraw-Hill 2001. Original purchasers of this book are permitted to photocopy or customize this page by downloading it from www.books.mcgraw-hill.com/training/download. The document can then be opened, edited, and printed using Microsoft Word or other word processing software.

Mini-Seminar 24

Selling to Groups: Group Presentation Dynamics

Objectives

1. To show participants how to tailor the Five Steps to Selling when groups are involved.

2. To teach participants how to build alliances quickly to increase sales.

Time Required

15–20 minutes

Materials Needed

- One copy of the activity sheet for each participant

- A flip chart or whiteboard

Directions for the Trainer

1. Read the lecturette prior to your training session, and take notes so you can use it as the basis for your own comments to the group.

2. Start the training session by taking a few minutes to deliver the lecturette in your own words. Then pass out copies of the activity sheet.

3. Activity Sheet 24-A: Organize the group into teams; select one of your products or services and an organization that is looking at a current proposal. Have participants identify who the stakeholders are within that organization and who falls into which of the three areas of the Ruck-Magee Customer Curve described in Mini-Seminar 16. Then discuss ways to engage that group to get a proposal on the fast track to acceptance.

LECTURETTE

When presenting a product or service solution to groups, the process is a more involved activity than presenting to one individual. With an increased number of decision makers involved in the process, the sales professional must analyze ahead of time the interest or lack of interest of each participant in the group Presentation.

A common habit of most sales professionals is to attempt to engage all participants in a group Presentation process from a generalized approach. This can result in the sales professional having to defend positions and statements that are challenged by one member of the group. In many instances, the group Presentation then becomes unmanageable.

You can prevent this from happening by mentally breaking the group down into the three subgroups that tend to be present in every group engagement. Each subgroup is manageable in its own way.

Rule 80/10/10

1. **Eighty percent** of the group tends to be neutral on issues. They wait to see which direction the momentum goes in, and then channel their commitments in the same direction. We label this group **Transmitters** of a norm. Transmitters choose a direction based on the influence of one of the other two subgroups.

2. **Ten percent** of any subgroup tends to be influencers in a forward, constructive direction. They are referred to as **Transformers**. They tend to transform a norm into greater yield.

3. **Ten percent** of any subgroup has the potential to be defeaters, complainers, challengers, or negativists. This group, labeled **Terrorists**, can derail the group Presentation and the possibility of any sale.

In most group Presentations, sales professionals may find themselves investing a disproportionate amount of time with Terrorists, and at the expense of forward momentum. When you engage the group, you are one lone percent factor, engaging 100 percent of the group, which makes you easy prey for the larger and seemingly more powerful 10 percent Terrorist group. Remember, the Transmitters channel their energies in the direction of the more formidable influencer subgroup. Terrorists are almost always eager to voice their views.. Transformers, on the other hand, will not share their views if they feel the environment is not safe or if they sense that the majority wants to go in the other direction.

Before any group sales Presentation, ask yourself which individuals have the capacity to fall into which subgroup when you engage them. Evaluate whether any Transformers are likely to be lined up behind your proposal. If not, then reschedule the timing of your group interaction. Gain support for your offer by engaging potential Transformers before the group engagement and getting buy-in from them. These individuals can then be used strategically in your sales Presentation to gain support and buy-in from the Transmitters. That will silence the Terrorists; they won't challenge you when they know you have a support network.

There are two ways in which you can analyze a group to determine which individuals have the greatest likelihood of being Transformers.

1. **Identify individuals you have a connection with:** people who you like, who you get along with, who are your friends, who like you, or who may owe you a favor.

2. **Identify individuals who have the most to gain by your offer based upon their** position, title, rank, age, sex, race, tenure with the organization, and so on. Look for what might interest them in your offer, and approach them from that perspective.

By approaching targeted Transformers prior to a group engagement and getting their buy-in (even if it's necessary to make some adjustments to the offer to gain that buy in), you can enter the group interaction with a support network.

Conversationally, you might start the group Presentation by saying something like this:

> "I would like to talk to you all about XYZ product. I have had the opportunity to visit with Susan, Tom, and Roger, and they think it's a good buy. Let me present the proposal and then get feedback from the group."

By strategically naming the people you have garnered support from, you draw in the Transmitters who follow any of those Transformers. At the same time, you have not put any one person on the spot by asking him or her to say anything publicly at the present time.

Selling to groups demands that the sales professional be comfortable with the Five Steps to Selling and strategically engage the group as a whole.

ACTIVITY SHEET 24-A
SELLING TO GROUPS: GROUP PRESENTATION DYNAMICS

PARTICIPANT'S
HANDOUT

Target Product or Service Offering: _____

_____

Targeted Organization or Client: _____

Identify Stakeholders of Each Subgroup by Name or Title:

_____

_____

_____

_____

_____

_____

_____

_____

_____

_____

_____

How You Would Engage This Group Based upon the Above Analysis:

_____

_____

_____

_____

_____

_____

_____

_____

_____

_____

_____

_____

_____

Copyright McGraw-Hill 2001. Original purchasers of this book are permitted to photocopy or customize this page by downloading it from www.books.mcgraw-hill.com/training/download. The document can then be opened, edited, and printed using Microsoft Word or other word processing software.

Objective

1. To teach participants how to tailor the Five Steps to Selling for culturally diverse buyers.

Time Required

15–20 minutes

Materials Needed

- One copy of the activity sheet for each participant

- A flip chart or whiteboard

Directions for the Trainer

1. Read the lecturette prior to your training session, and take notes so you can use it as the basis for your own comments to the group.

2. Start the training session by taking a few minutes to deliver the lecturette in your own words. Then pass out copies of the activity sheets.

3. Activity Sheet 25-A: Organize the group into teams and have them discuss what they feel are important factors in selling to differing ethnic groups. Debrief by asking several participants to share their thoughts. With the group, develop a list of action items for becoming more culturally sensitive and perceptive.

Mini-Seminar 25

Selling to Culturally Diverse Audiences

LECTURETTE

In a world of political correctness and hypersensitivity to others, many sales Presentations are nevertheless sabotaged by sales professionals themselves who fail to recognize the necessity for making cultural adjustments when presenting to culturally varied customers. It is critical that sales professionals learn the do's and don'ts of engaging others who may be of different ethnic or cultural backgrounds than themselves.

Ms. Lenora Billings-Harris, a leading diversity expert, talks of four approaches to gain a better understanding of diversity issues:

1. Knowledge—Learn the customers' ways and especially their language. The language will direct you to what that cultural group holds important.

2. Understanding—Read books, watch videos, and go where they go to learn their ways, values, and beliefs.

3. Acceptance—Accept them on the terms on which they want to be accepted. The Golden Rule doesn't always apply in diversity matters; how you may want to be accepted may be in violation of something that is held sacred by the other group.

4. Behavior—Match your behavior to theirs.

In working with and selling to culturally diverse groups, your words, mannerisms, nonverbal communication signals, sales materials, and how the relationship is managed must all be altered to suit the group being engaged. For example, many individuals of Asian descent view a smile in a business transaction as disrespectful, whereas in the United States smiling during the selling transaction is the norm, and is a way of expressing appreciation. Thus, a collision of cultures can cause a selling nightmare.

ACTIVITY SHEET 25-A
SELLING TO CULTURALLY DIVERSE AUDIENCES

PARTICIPANT'S HANDOUT

Target Product or Service Offering: _____

_____

Target an Ethnic Demographic: _____

Identify Differing Factors That Can Make or Break a Selling Transaction: _____

_____

_____

_____

_____

_____

_____

_____

_____

_____

_____

How You Can Bounce Back from an "Oops": _____

_____

_____

_____

_____

_____

_____

_____

_____

_____

_____

Copyright McGraw-Hill 2001. Original purchasers of this book are permitted to photocopy or customize this page by downloading it from www.books.mcgraw-hill.com/training/download. The document can then be opened, edited, and printed using Microsoft Word or other word processing software.

Mini-Seminar 26

Differentiating Your Offer via Unique Selling Features/USF #1

Objective

1. To help participants recognize that the more knowledge they have about the products or services they represent, the greater their ability to motivate a prospect or customer to buy.

Time Required

10–15 minutes

Materials Needed

- One copy of each of the two activity sheets for each participant

- A flip chart or whiteboard

- A book of matches

Directions for the Trainer

1. Read the lecturette prior to your training session, and take notes so you can use it as the basis for your own comments to the group.

2. Start the training session by taking a few minutes to deliver the lecturette in your own words. Then pass out a book of matches for every few participants.

3. Activity Sheet 26-A: Have each participant strike a match and hold it in her hands. While it is lit, the sales professional must recite as many different products or services as she can. See how many items they can recite while under the pressure of the flame, before they either run out of items to list or have to blow out the match. Keep score and see who knows the most.

4. Activity Sheet 26-B: Now have each sales professional select a product or service of her choice, strike a second match, and while it is lit, recite as many Facts or Features as she can about that one product or service. Again, see who readily knows the most and can recite it the quickest.

LECTURETTE

Differentiating your offer based on the tangibles is a hallmark trait of successful sales professionals. Marketing researchers have found that organizations or persons can differentiate themselves in a marketplace by examining two Unique Selling Features (USF). The first USF is examined in this mini-seminar; the second is presented in Mini-Seminar 27.

> Unique Selling Feature #1 identifies all of the specific factors that you offer and that your competition does not. In essence, USF #1 centers on all the things you offer, the "what" factors, the tangibles.

Many times in the marketplace a prospect or customer may have a difficult time seeing the true differentiators, understanding what you offer as being genuinely different from what others offer. In that case, your offer may blend into the sea of options, instead of standing out as the first choice among options and offers.

Sales professionals must recognize the importance of having a depth of knowledge of all the unique things they represent. Knowing all of the unique "what" factors allows the sales professional to make an informed, educated Presentation to prospects or customers. If you have limited knowledge of the totality of "what" factors, then you will miss many selling opportunities.

Burger King restaurant chain differentiates itself in advertisements by using USF #1 when it says:

> "Our burgers are *flame-broiled*!"

This statement differentiates Burger King in the sea of fast-food hamburger options by communicating to the customers in their marketplace that its USF is better.

Ask yourself if you have a Unique Selling Feature that is as stand-alone and powerful as that USF jingle, which has been used for decades!

ACTIVITY SHEET 26-A
DIFFERENTIATING YOUR OFFER VIA UNIQUE
SELLING FEATURE (USF) #1

Recite as many as you can of the different products or services you can provide to a prospect or customer, while you hold a lit match. See how many items you readily know. Make this a fun, fast game to illustrate your ability to instantly draw upon your working knowledge of what you represent while under pressure.

Copyright McGraw-Hill 2001. Original purchasers of this book are permitted to photocopy or customize this page by downloading it from www.books.mcgraw-hill.com/training/download. The document can then be opened, edited, and printed using Microsoft Word or other word processing software.

Now select a specific product or service that you feel most knowledgeable about. Recite as many different facts or features as you can that specifically relate to that single item, while you hold a lit match. See how many specific facts or features you readily know. Make this a fun, fast game to illustrate your ability to instantly draw upon your working knowledge of a single product or service while under pressure.

Copyright McGraw-Hill 2001. Original purchasers of this book are permitted to photocopy or customize this page by downloading it from www.books.mcgraw-hill.com/training/download. The document can then be opened, edited, and printed using Microsoft Word or other word processing software.

Objective

1. To help participants recognize that the more knowledge they have of the products or services they represent, the greater their ability will be to motivate customers to buy.

Time Required

10–15 minutes

Materials Needed

- One copy of each of the two activity sheets for each participant

- A flip chart or whiteboard

- A book of matches

Directions for the Trainer

1. Read the lecturette prior to your training session, and take notes so you can use it as the basis for your own comments to the group.

2. Start the training session by taking a few minutes to deliver the lecturette in your own words. Then pass out a book of matches for every few participants.

3. Activity Sheet 27-A: Have each participant strike a match and hold it in his hands. While it is lit, the sales professional should recite as many different values or Benefits to doing business with your organization as he can. See how many USF #2's participants can recite while under the pressure of the flame, before either running out of items to say or having to blow out the match. Keep score and see who knows the most.

4. Activity Sheet 27-B: Now have each sales professional select a product or service of his choice, strike a second match, and while it is lit, recite as many Values or Benefits as he can about that one product or service. Again, see who readily knows the most and recites it the quickest.

Mini-Seminar 27

Differentiating Your Offer via Unique Service Features (USF) #2

LECTURETTE

Differentiating your offers by the way in which you make the offer or by what the offer does is another hallmark trait of successful sales professionals.

While marketing research indicates that organizations or persons can differentiate themselves in a marketplace by examining their Unique Selling Features (USF), the selling world has also learned that sometimes an even greater differentiator is the sales professional's Unique Service Feature (USF) #2!

> Unique Service Feature/USF #2 identifies all the unique ways in which you deliver your offer or the unique ways in which your product does what it does. In essence, USF #2 centers on all the ways your product delivers or performs, the "how" factors, the value it delivers.

Many times in the marketplace a prospect or customer may have a difficult time seeing "how" the differentiators perform as being genuinely different from "how" others perform. When that happens, your offer may blend into the sea of options, instead of standing out as the first choice among options and offers.

Sales professionals must recognize the importance of having a depth of knowledge of all the unique things they represent. Knowing all of the unique "how" factors allows the sales professional to make an informed, educated Presentation to prospects or customers. If you have limited knowledge of the "how" factors, then you will miss many selling opportunities.

BurgerKing's restaurant chain differentiates itself in advertisements by using a USF #2 when it says:

> "Hold the pickles, hold the lettuce, special orders don't upset us, have it **your way**!"

This statement differentiates BurgerKing's in the sea of fast-food hamburger options by communicating to the customers in their marketplace that their USF is your USF.

Ask yourself if you have a Unique Service Feature that is as stand-alone and powerful as that USF jingle, which has been used for decades!

ACTIVITY SHEET 27-A
DIFFERENTIATING YOUR OFFER VIA UNIQUE
SELLING FEATURES (USF) #2

Organization: Recite as many different values or benefits as you can that your organization can provide to a prospect or customer, while you hold a lit match. See how many unique "how" factors you readily know. Make this a fun, fast game to illustrate your ability to instantly draw upon your working knowledge of what you represent while under pressure.

Copyright McGraw-Hill 2001. Original purchasers of this book are permitted to photocopy or customize this page by downloading it from www.books.mcgraw-hill.com/training/download. The document can then be opened, edited, and printed using Microsoft Word or other word processing software.

ACTIVITY SHEET 27-B
DIFFERENTIATING YOUR OFFER VIA UNIQUE
SELLING FEATURES (USF) #2

Now select a specific product or service that you feel most knowledgeable about. Recite as many different values or benefits that specifically relate to that single item as you can, while you hold a lit match. See how many specific "how" statements you readily know. Make this a fun, fast game to illustrate your ability to instantly draw upon your working knowledge of a single product or service while under pressure.

Copyright McGraw-Hill 2001. Original purchasers of this book are permitted to photocopy or customize this page by downloading it from www.books.mcgraw-hill.com/training/download. The document can then be opened, edited, and printed using Microsoft Word or other word processing software.

Objectives

1. To teach participants to always be addressing one or a combination of the four differentiators in the market between themselves and someone else.

2. To illustrate for participants that every sales offer addresses one of the four essential differentiators.

Time Required

10–15 minutes

Materials Needed

- One copy of each of the two activity sheets for each participant

- A flip chart or whiteboard

- A stack of blank index cards

Directions for the Trainer

1. Read the lecturette prior to your training session, and take notes so you can use it as the basis for your own comments to the group.

2. Start the training session by taking a few minutes to deliver the lecturette in your own words. Then ask participants to form teams, and pass out eight blank index cards to each team.

3. Activity Sheet 28-A: Have the teams each complete a set of cards for the Organization and a set for the most profitable product or service that you offer. Determine which team listed the largest number of viable responses for each card, and ask those teams to share their results with the whole group.

4. Activity Sheet 28-B: Have participants practice with one another, using the cards as their talking points in a role-playing selling situation.

Mini-Seminar 28

Showing the Customer How Your Offer Excels

LECTURETTE

No matter how many decisions a customer has to make when going through the selling process, or how many decision makers are listening to the sales professional's Presentation, there are four ways in which a sales professional can make her offer stand apart from others.

Every time you make a Presentation, conduct a demonstration, or engage in a sales dialogue with another person, everything you do must be done in such a way that it addresses one or a combination of the differentiators that consumers consider when making buying decisions.

We make decisions based upon a product or service being:

Better than the competition or other choices.

Faster than the competition or other choices.

Uniquely different from the competition or other choices.

More cost-effective than the competition or other choices.

Evaluate every piece of sales literature you use, every comment you make, all the advertisements placed by your organization, and all the Features you present in the selling process to make sure that they all speak to one of the four key differentiators.

There is nothing truly new in life. There are only adaptations, improvements, adjustment, modifications, and so on of existing products and services. As a result, sales professionals have to examine what you represent and ask yourselves how your product or service compels another person to select your offer over other offers. Ask yourself:

"How does my offer do something either Better, Faster, Differently, or more Cost-Effectively than anything else?"

Successful selling involves communicating to prospects or customers how your offer will be best for them, based upon its unique quality of being Better, Faster, Different, or more Cost-Effective.

ACTIVITY SHEET 28-A
SHOWING THE CUSTOMER HOW YOUR OFFER EXCELS

Organization:

In a team, take four cards from a stack of blank index cards and label each card with one of the four differentiators (Better, Faster, Different, More Cost-Effective). Brainstorm as many responses for each card as you can, as it relates to the organization you represent in the marketplace when compared to the competition.

Report to the whole group the number of responses your team had for each of the four cards. Discuss some of the responses to ensure that the differentiators your team listed are truly unique to your organization and that the competition couldn't say the same thing(s).

Product or Service: _____.

In a team, take four cards from a stack of blank index cards and label each card with one of the four differentiators (Better, Faster, Different, More Cost-Effective). Brainstorm as many responses for each card as you can, as it relates to that product or service you represent in the marketplace when compared to the competition.

Report to the whole group the number of responses your team had for each of the four cards. Discuss some of the responses to ensure that the differentiators your team listed are truly unique to your product or service and that the competition couldn't say the same thing(s).

Copyright McGraw-Hill 2001. Original purchasers of this book are permitted to photocopy or customize this page by downloading it from www.books.mcgraw-hill.com/training/download. The document can then be opened, edited, and printed using Microsoft Word or other word processing software.

Organization:

In a team, take the four cards that you have labeled with the four differentiators (Better, Faster, Different, More Cost-Effective). Role-play a sales Presentation, using those statements in a conversational way with a hypothetical prospect or customer.

Product or Service: _____.

In a team, take the four cards that you have labeled with the four differentiators (Better, Faster, Different, More Cost-Effective). Role-play a sales Presentation, using those statements in a conversational way with a hypothetical prospect or customer.

Copyright McGraw-Hill 2001. Original purchasers of this book are permitted to photocopy or customize this page by downloading it from www.books.mcgraw-hill.com/training/download. The document can then be opened, edited, and printed using Microsoft Word or other word processing software.

Mini-Seminar 29

Seven Steps to Improved Listening Skills

Objective

1. To show participants multiple ways to improve their listening ability, reduce their tendency to interrupt or not listen intently enough, and become better solution providers.

Time Required

10–15 minutes

Materials Needed

- One copy of each of the two activity sheets for each participant

- A flip chart or whiteboard

Directions for the Trainer

1. Read the lecturette prior to your training session, and take notes so you can use it as the basis for your own comments to the group.

2. Start the training session by taking a few minutes to deliver the lecturette in your own words. Then pass out the activity sheets to every participant.

3. Activity 29-A: Have participants come up with as many listening techniques as they can, one for each letter. Then have them pair off into teams to share and expand their lists. Now, bring the teams back together and debrief by asking some of the teams to share their ideas with the group.

4. Activity 28-B: Have participants brainstorm actual ways to improve their listening skills, and ways to coach one another nonconfrontationally to embrace, accept, and perform some of these techniques in the workplace. Debrief by asking some of the participants to share their action plans with the group. You may want to combine all the ideas generated in this activity, transcribe them to one activity sheet, and make a poster of Sales Professionals' Commitment Steps for improved listening ability, for teams to refer to after the mini-seminar.

155

LECTURETTE

It is said that the greatest ability a person can have is the ability to listen to another person and do so without interrupting. This is even more true for a sales professional.

Sales professionals must be practiced in the art of listening to the verbal and nonverbal language of the other person. It is difficult to listen to another person if one's focus is not on that other person, if there are distractions, hidden agendas, frustrations, or a desire to get through with the conversation and move on to another person or task.

Listening takes conscious effort. Making effective Presentations and increasing sales effectiveness result from your ability to listen to the other person. Through listening, you can learn much about another person, including:

1. how he thinks (logically or emotionally);

2. his immediate needs;

3. his future needs;

4. his past experiences with you, your firm, or other sales professionals; and

5. the common ground the two of you share.

The following acronym will help sales professionals remember a number of techniques for improving their listening skills.

> **L = Look and listen:** Make sure nonverbal signals are consistent with verbal signals.

> **I = Implied interest:** If you show that you are genuinely interested, the other party will become more comfortable with you, more relaxed, and thus more engaged.

> **S = Summarize key points often:** Solicit feedback to ensure that you are listening correctly and, conversely, that the points you make have value to the other person.

> **T = Territorial sensitivity:** Respect the other person's space, knowledge, beliefs, age, race, sex, profession, and station in life. Violating any of these territories may cause the other person to tune you out. Likewise, if the other person violates your territory, you may want to stop listening. Force yourself to listen; set aside what has offended you and focus on listening.

> **E = Empathetic position:** You must be empathetic to what the other person says. Empathy implies that you understand; it doesn't imply that you agree, or that one person is right or wrong!

> **N = Names, notes and nonverbal signals:** Here are three ways to use the letter "N" as a listening technology tool. Using people's names in the conversation and in correspondence serves as a magnet to pull them in and keep the dialogue personal. Note-taking is a powerful tool for keeping control over one's mouth—if you have a tendency to talk too much or interrupt others, start carrying a note pad and, when the other person talks, take

notes. It is physically impossible to write notes and talk coherently at the same time. Finally, watching the other person's nonverbal signals can provide powerful information.

S = Smile: Smiling (not smirking) makes people warm up to you.

Far too many sales are lost because the sales professional talked too much. Far too many sales are lost because the sales professional did not listen effectively.

ACTIVITY 29-A
SEVEN STEPS TO IMPROVED LISTENING SKILLS

Listening improvement requires conscious effort by sales professionals.
Some of the ways to significantly improve your listening ability are:

Individual Ideas		Team Ideas
_____	L	_____
_____	–	_____
_____	I	_____
_____	–	_____
_____	S	_____
_____	–	_____
_____	T	_____
_____	–	_____
_____	E	_____
_____	–	_____
_____	N	_____
_____	–	_____
_____	S	_____
_____	–	_____

Copyright McGraw-Hill 2001. Original purchasers of this book are permitted to photocopy or customize this page by downloading it from www.books.mcgraw-hill.com/training/download. The document can then be opened, edited, and printed using Microsoft Word or other word processing software.

ACTIVITY 29-B
SEVEN STEPS TO IMPROVED LISTENING SKILLS

PARTICIPANT'S
HANDOUT

Listening improvement requires conscious effort by sales professionals. For each of the tools you identified in Activity 29-A, now develop specific plans to put each into action in a sales dialogue with a prospect or customer or with colleagues.

Application Ideas for the LISTENS Model

L _____

_____

I _____

_____

S _____

_____

T _____

_____

E _____

_____

N _____

_____

S _____

_____

Copyright McGraw-Hill 2001. Original purchasers of this book are permitted to photocopy or customize this page by downloading it from www.books.mcgraw-hill.com/training/download. The document can then be opened, edited, and printed using Microsoft Word or other word processing software.

Mini-Seminar 30

Improving Your Communication Effectiveness: Sending the Correct Signal

Objective

1. To help participants recognize how they may have inadvertently offended prospects or customers in their communication exchanges.

Time Required

15–20 minutes

Materials Needed

- One copy of the activity sheet for each participant

- A flip chart or whiteboard

Directions for the Trainer

1. Read the lecturette below prior to your training session, and take notes so you can use it as the basis for your own comments to the group.

2. Start the training session by taking a few minutes to deliver the lecturette in your own words. Then pass out copies of the activity sheet to every participant.

3. Activity 30-A: Have participants team up in groups of 3 to 5. Each participant will have a turn as the speaker, while others play the role of listeners. Each participant is instructed to share a story with the members of the group. Speakers can talk about anything they want (what they did over the weekend, what they are going to do for the coming weekend, their favorite hobby, their last successful selling situation, etc.).

The task is to tell your story to the other members of the group until all listeners feel that they have connected to the speaker. The listeners will raise their hands in the air and, when they feel the speaker has made eye contact with them for a minimum of five seconds, the listeners will telegraph that they have been connected by lowering their hands. The speaker must continue the story until all hands are down in the team. Then a second speaker takes a turn, and the exercise continues until all participants have had a chance to play the speaker.

Debrief with the group by asking whether it was simple or challenging to try to talk coherently while making a connection with each listener.

LECTURETTE

Communication studies abound, and while one report indicates that certain components within a communication exchange influence the interpretation by the receiving party, another study says the opposite. However, all communication experts agree on three points:

1. A portion of one's interpretation of a communication exchange is influenced solely by *what* has been said.

2. A portion of one's interpretation of a communication exchange is influenced solely by *why* the words have been said.

3. A portion of one's interpretation of a communication exchange is influenced solely by *how* the words have been said.

Sales professionals must recognize that choosing precisely what words and message to send is critical. The exact words exchanged are used by the listener for cognitively understanding the message. But the words themselves also make up the portion of the exchange that typically registers second overall.

The listener will put the message into its proper perspective based upon the supporting components perceived—why the exchange is taking place and the urgency of the message. These parts of the exchange are communicated to the listener through nonverbal signals; nonverbals are more powerful influencers of the interpretation of the exchange than are the actual words spoken.

Ineffective communication exchanges are often the result of ineffective transmission of nonverbal signals. What the human ear registers before registering words is how the words are spoken. How you speak includes:

1. tone of voice,

2. pitch,

3. pace,

4. volume,

5. accent, and

6. intonation.

Sales professionals must realize that while they may spend significant time working on exactly what to say to a prospect or customer, they must also pay attention to how the words will be delivered.

ACTIVITY 30-A
IMPROVING YOUR COMMUNICATION EFFECTIVENESS:
SENDING THE CORRECT SIGNAL

In teams of 3 to 5, take turns sharing a short story.

Roles: Speaker shares a story with the listeners. Listeners all hold one hand in the air as a signal that they are listening, and keep their hands up until they feel the speaker has communicated directly to them for five uninterrupted seconds.

Listeners will score the speaker after all hands are down.

Speaker 1: _____

(ineffective) -5 -4 -3 -2 -1   What Factors   1+ 2+ 3+ 4+ 5+ (effective)

(ineffective) -5 -4 -3 -2 -1   Why Factors   1+ 2+ 3+ 4+ 5+ (effective)

(ineffective) -5 -4 -3 -2 -1   How Factors   1+ 2+ 3+ 4+ 5+ (effective)

Speaker 2: _____

(ineffective) -5 -4 -3 -2 -1   What Factors   1+ 2+ 3+ 4+ 5+ (effective)

(ineffective) -5 -4 -3 -2 -1   Why Factors   1+ 2+ 3+ 4+ 5+ (effective)

(ineffective) -5 -4 -3 -2 -1   How Factors   1+ 2+ 3+ 4+ 5+ (effective)

Speaker 3: _____

(ineffective) -5 -4 -3 -2 -1   What Factors   1+ 2+ 3+ 4+ 5+ (effective)

(ineffective) -5 -4 -3 -2 -1   Why Factors   1+ 2+ 3+ 4+ 5+ (effective)

(ineffective) -5 -4 -3 -2 -1   How Factors   1+ 2+ 3+ 4+ 5+ (effective)

Speaker 4: _____

(ineffective) -5 -4 -3 -2 -1   What Factors   1+ 2+ 3+ 4+ 5+ (effective)

(ineffective) -5 -4 -3 -2 -1   Why Factors   1+ 2+ 3+ 4+ 5+ (effective)

(ineffective) -5 -4 -3 -2 -1   How Factors   1+ 2+ 3+ 4+ 5+ (effective)

Speaker 5: _____

(ineffective) -5 -4 -3 -2 -1   What Factors   1+ 2+ 3+ 4+ 5+ (effective)

(ineffective) -5 -4 -3 -2 -1   Why Factors   1+ 2+ 3+ 4+ 5+ (effective)

(ineffective) -5 -4 -3 -2 -1   How Factors   1+ 2+ 3+ 4+ 5+ (effective)

Copyright McGraw-Hill 2001. Original purchasers of this book are permitted to photocopy or customize this page by downloading it from www.books.mcgraw-hill.com/training/download. The document can then be opened, edited, and printed using Microsoft Word or other word processing software.

Professional-Level Selling Skills

Objective

1. To help participants accelerate their selling abilities by maximizing prime selling time and stimulating inbound contacts from targeted prospects or customers.

Time Required

15–20 minutes

Materials Needed

- One copy of the activity sheet for each participant

- A flip chart or whiteboard

- Participants' daily planner systems (Day Planner, DayRunner, Franklin Planner, DayTimer, note paper, To-Do list, etc.)

Directions for the Trainer

1. Read the lecturette prior to your training session, and take notes so you can use it as the basis for your own comments to the group.

2. Start the training session by summarizing the lecturette in your own words; then pass out the activity sheets.

3. Activity Sheet 31-A: Have participants identify three contact categories that might contain 50 or more contacts each—a Suspect pool, a Prospect pool, and a Customer pool. Then have them draft an offer for each category that can be developed into a letter, e-mail message, faxable gram, or voice mail message to be used after the session.

Using Rule 1/12/50 to Continually Connect

LECTURETTE

Great sales professionals aren't born successful. Planned work and daily efforts lead to the consistent sales that allow them to be perceived by others as great. Sales professionals must learn to recognize the daily efforts that can assist in generating inquiries from targeted demographics. Those Inquiries can result in sales Presentations and subsequent Closed sales.

During the downtime in the sales day, your schedule should be dominated by productive, constructive activities.

Most sales professionals would rather have their teeth pulled without pain-numbing medicines than make cold calls on a daily basis. One way to turn cold calls into warm calls is to deploy Rule 1/12/50. Rule 1/12/50 will stimulate inbound inquiries about your services or products; let you reach out to never-before-contacted suspects or prospects and introduce yourself to them in a nonthreatening manner; and ensure that your Sales Funnel (see Mini-Seminar 14) always remains full of leads.

What is Rule 1/12/50? It is a systematic approach to selling that employs manageable marketing efforts. Regardless of any other efforts being initiated by your organization, you can increase your sales using Rule 1/12/50.

Rule 1/12/50

1 = Represents actions that should take place the first part of every month. Whether that is day one or the first days of the first week of each month, make it work for your schedule.

12 = Represents a consistent approach to be used for all 12 months of the year before any analysis is undertaken as to whether to continue the approach, stop the approach, or adjust the approach.

50 = Represents the targeted number of outbound contacts to be initiated every month. Identify the best 50 suspects you want to introduce yourself to, the best 50 prospects you want to make a specific offer to, and the best 50 customers (active or inactive) you want to give a Presentation to.

The specific contact action is a personalized direct marketing approach. That monthly action can be:

1. A handwritten note in a hand-addressed envelope. (Studies reveal that handwritten envelopes are opened first in a stack of mail, and that handwritten notes are read from beginning to end, not scanned!) Always include several of your business cards!

2. A personal letter with a suggested use for one of your products or services that the prospect may not be aware of. Always include several of your business cards!

3. An e-mail announcement, offer, or request.

4. A fax-gram and a fax-back response request form for more information or requested follow-up.

5. A direct mail card announcing who you are or something great that is now available and specifying ways to contact you to find out more.

6. A copy of any press releases or press clippings that may serve to stimulate the prospect to contact you for more information.

Brainstorm with your colleagues differing ways to contact suspects, prospects, and customers. Also brainstorm powerful messages to include in your communication.

Now cold calls become warm calls. A sales professional can now make an outbound call to a suspect, prospect, or customer, and the call might go like this:

"Hello, this is _____ with _____. I recently sent you a note on _____. Have you had the opportunity to read it?"

1. If the answer is yes, then proceed with your conversational sales process.

2. If the answer is no, then say, "That's all right; the reason I sent it to you is . . . ."

Rule 1/12/50 helps you to fill your Sales Funnel with contacts at all three levels; it may stimulate some contacts to call you; and it may even add to your bottom line, all from a simple letter and a postage stamp. Low-cost marketing, high-yield sales.

ACTIVITY 31-A
USING RULE 1/12/50 TO CONTINUALLY CONNECT

Complement your selling efforts by designing a direct marketing contact campaign to continually feed your **Sales Funnel** using **Rule 1/12/50.**

Identify specific industries, markets, geographies, groups, associations, types of individuals, and so on that you can direct your letters, faxes, or e-mails to on a monthly basis:

	Suspect Pool	Prospect Pool	Customer Pool
Month One:	_____	_____	_____
Month Two:	_____	_____	_____
Month Three:	_____	_____	_____
Month Four:	_____	_____	_____
Month Five:	_____	_____	_____
Month Six:	_____	_____	_____
Month Seven:	_____	_____	_____
Month Eight:	_____	_____	_____
Month Nine:	_____	_____	_____
Month Ten:	_____	_____	_____
Month Eleven:	_____	_____	_____
Month Twelve:	_____	_____	_____

*Transpose each of the monthly action plans above to your personal calendar system, on the first week of each corresponding month. This will assist in motivating you to take action!

Month One Offer: _____

Month Two Offer: _____

Month Three Offer: _____

Month Four Offer: _____

Month Five Offer: _____

Month Six Offer: _____

Month Seven Offer: _____

Month Eight Offer: _____

Month Nine Offer: _____

Month Ten Offer: _____

Month Eleven Offer: _____

Month Twelve Offer: _____

Month One Specific Offer in Text Form: _____

_____

Copyright McGraw-Hill 2001. Original purchasers of this book are permitted to photocopy or customize this page by downloading it from www.books.mcgraw-hill.com/training/download. The document can then be opened, edited, and printed using Microsoft Word or other word processing software.

Mini-Seminar 32

Leveraging Existing Relationships for More Business

Objectives

1. To help participants mine existing account relationships for greater business partnerships and cultivate additional business prospects with each contact.

2. To help participants analyze existing accounts to determine whether existing clients are utilizing all available product or service lines.

Time Required

15–20 minutes

Materials Needed

- One copy of the activity sheet for each participant

- A flip chart or whiteboard

- Participants' lists of their top three active customers and a list of all products or services those customers have purchased over the past three years.

Directions for the Trainer

1. Read the lecturette prior to your training session, and take notes so you can use it as the basis for your own comments to the group.

2. Start the training session by summarizing the lecturette in your own words; then pass out the activity sheets.

3. Activity Sheet 32-A: Have participants complete the customer analysis form and then pair off. Pairs will discuss each other's three clients and the products being used, and strategize ways to Present other complementary products or services to the customers for consideration. Pairs will also discuss whether there could be other purchasing powers (other work units, departments, divisions, people) within that client's organization that you are not presently contacting, but that the client could introduce you to for increased sales opportunities.

LECTURETTE

Sales professionals must recognize whether they mine for more business with existing clients, or whether they have become complacent and act as account managers, merely taking orders from customers without trying to meet all of their product or service needs.

The fastest way to increase sales volumes is to start with existing clients, especially satisfied customers. Sales professionals often fail to see the totality of business opportunities that every individual client represents. It is a simple matter to examine all the products or services you offer and match them up against the sales you have made to each customer.

Train yourself to ask enough questions of existing clients so you can determine what products or services in your lineup of offerings will address the client's immediate needs. Also determine what products or services in your lineup of offerings will be necessary for the client to go from where she is today to where she says she wants to be one day.

By knowing a client's short-term and long-term goals, you can serve as a consultant, guiding the client toward smarter purchasing decisions, increased purchasing decisions, and more profitable purchasing decisions. A powerful way to gain this insight is to read your client's Mission Statement. It will tell you what the client deems important and where the client is going!

It takes much more time to find a new suspect, convert the suspect into a prospect, entice the prospect to hear a sales Presentation, and work for the new customer than to cultivate more business from existing clients!

Aside from expanding the level or volume of sales of your products or services to current clients, another way to cultivate additional business from existing clients is to utilize them as conduits to other buyers within the same organization, town, family, group, and so on.

Brainstorm with your colleagues, using one of your organization's existing clients as an example. See how many other potential buyers could be reached through that one point of contact that you are not presently in dialogue with. Leverage the existing relationship between you and the organization in contacting the new potential buying contacts; that relationship helps them to see you as a credible option.

Sales professionals can dramatically increase their sales effectiveness by cultivating or mining existing client relationships for additional business opportunities, while at the same time focusing their efforts on looking for new clients.

ACTIVITY 32-A
LEVERAGING EXISTING RELATIONSHIPS FOR
MORE BUSINESS

PARTICIPANT'S
HANDOUT

Identify and analyze your top three revenue-generating clients to determine if you can leverage that existing relationship for additional sales opportunities by offering other products or services.

Client One: _____

Primary Product or Service Buying: _____

Complementary Offer: _____

Client Two: _____

Primary Product or Service Buying: _____

Complementary Offer: _____

Client Three: _____

Primary Product or Service Buying: _____

Complementary Offer: _____

Now analyze Client One to determine if there are business units or purchasing powers that you could be contacting that you either have never contacted or have not contacted in some time. They could be:

Client One: _____

Primary Product or Service Buying: _____

Other Products or Services Being Bought Now or in the Past: _____

_____

_____

Based upon my experience, other buyers of this same product outside of this client typically are (think in terms of work units, departments, ethnicity or gender trends, geographical trends of purchasing patterns, buyer's titles or positions, other industry buyers, other businesses that buy, etc.): _____

_____

_____

_____

_____

_____

_____

*Now circle all of the above types of buyers that your existing client organizations have within them, but that you are not presently in dialogue with. Go for them!

Copyright McGraw-Hill 2001. Original purchasers of this book are permitted to photocopy or customize this page by downloading it from www.books.mcgraw-hill.com/training/download. The document can then be opened, edited, and printed using Microsoft Word or other word processing software.

Objective

1. To help participants realize that their best advocates are their present happy customers, who can be treasure chests of potential new prospects and customers.

Time Required

15–20 minutes

Materials Needed

- One copy of the activity sheet for each participant

- A flip chart or whiteboard

Directions for the Trainer

1. Read the lecturette prior to your training session, and take notes so you can use it as the basis for your own comments to the group.

2. Start the training session by summarizing the lecturette in your own words; then pass out the activity sheets.

3. Activity Sheet 33-A: Have participants identify ways to get customer endorsements, ways to leverage those endorsements, and ways to solicit referrals from customers. Instruct them to use the activity sheet as a template to identify what top business customers are doing presently that may cause them to be good candidates for soliciting referrals from; or which of your client relationships may allow you to encourage customers to give you referrals in the future. Then discuss best ideas and design action plans that each sales professional will commit to after the session for approaching their top twenty customers.

Mini-Seminar 33

Getting Referrals from Every Client

LECTURETTE

Studies show that it takes significantly more time, energy, and money to solicit new business from individuals and organizations that are not presently doing business with you than it takes to develop more business from existing customers. With all of the evidence to support this, it is still the norm for sales professionals to look at the business stream as primarily coming from new clients and to focus their energy on finding new clients.

While new clients are the lifeblood of any business, maintaining healthy, productive relationships with existing clients will do more for building a solid business base and ensuring positive revenue streams.

Review their present business activities to answer these questions:

1. What percentage of my work is centered on cultivating additional business from existing clients? _____%

2. What percentage of my work is centered on getting to know existing clients to either ask them for referrals or allow for the client to give me referrals? _____%

3. What percentage of my work is centered on building my business base by identifying and working to get new clients? _____%

These are powerful questions to ask yourself. The answers will help you to determine if you have been leaving money on the table—a term used for not actively working every account so that you do all the business possible with them.

The best way to build customer loyalty is to take care of customers' immediate needs and do the same for their close friends and business associates—it makes them look good and endears you to them.

Learn to recognize the most opportune time in a sales transaction to hint, suggest, or request that a satisfied customer give you referrals.

Referrals can come in many ways:

1. **Verbal recommendation to call someone specific**—Get the name at the precise moment it is offered; write it down along with a few quick facts about the prospect. (Refer to the Stacking-N-Linking model in Mini-Seminar 11 to be sure you ask the types of questions that will allow you to learn more about the referred contact.)

2. **E-mail, telephone, written options**—When a suggested name is given, request that the customer send the referral information to you via one of these channels. You can always follow up with the customer afterward via the same channel to remind the customer of the offer to make a referral. Reminder: It is acceptable to remind a customer of an offer to refer you to someone, but don't hassle the customer.

3. **Victory letter**—Ask the customer who sings your praises to put those words into a letter for you to share with other potential customers. As you are having this dialogue, transition into a subtle question: "Are there people you know who I should send copies of your letter to?"

4. **Customer literature**—Find out whether the customer has any organizational printed materials in which they list benefits or accomplishments for their customers to know about, which you in turn participated in. Ask them to reference your name (personal or business) or include a picture of you (personal or business), and then get a copy for your selling portfolio.

When you receive letters of praise, use these positive words about you as supplements to any mailers you send (see Mini-Seminar 31, on Rule 1/12/50), to display in wall hangings or display books on tables, to use as reprints, to include in newsletters or fax-grams, and so on.

Sometimes the best silent sales assistants a sales professional can have are words of praise from a satisfied customer. Leverage those words with people who directly know the customer in question. A second way to leverage these words is to identify all like points of contact to the customer and place the words in front of them.

A great way to complete the sales cycle is to send every customer, regardless of the amount of the transaction, a follow-up handwritten thank-you note and include in it an extra business card (with permission to share the business card with someone the customer knows). Include in the note a simple request to call you with the name(s) of anyone you should contact. Every one of these contacts will not yield feedback, but many will; and every one *will* leave a customer with one more positive impression of you as a sales professional!

ACTIVITY 33-A
GETTING REFERRALS FROM EVERY CLIENT

Identify your top twenty customers and make a note about how best to approach each of them for referrals.

	Client	Best Approach
1.		
2.		
3.		
4.		
5.		
6.		
7.		
8.		
9.		
10.		
11.		
12.		
13.		
14.		
15.		
16.		
17.		
18.		
19.		
20.		

*Quickly scan your Rolodex, database file, and collection of client business cards to see how many people you should contact immediately.

Copyright McGraw-Hill 2001. Original purchasers of this book are permitted to photocopy or customize this page by downloading it from www.books.mcgraw-hill.com/training/download. The document can then be opened, edited, and printed using Microsoft Word or other word processing software.

Objective

1. To teach participants how to complement their existing efforts by cultivating additional business from sources most sales professionals fail to look at—past and lost accounts!

Time Required

15–20 minutes

Materials Needed

- One copy of the activity sheet for each participant

- A flip chart or whiteboard

- Participants' own lists of inactive clients, or a list of inactive clients of the organization to be assigned or reassigned to participants

Directions for the Trainer

1. Read the lecturette prior to your training session, and take notes so you can use it as the basis for your own comments to the group.

2. Start the training session by summarizing the lecturette in your own words; then pass out the activity sheets.

3. Activity Sheet 34-A: Have participants identify three inactive clients either by industry, geographical region, size, age, Standard Industry Code (SIC number), sales volume, or other affinity factor, and then run the BLENDS model on each client to determine a best course of action for contacting each inactive account.

Mini-Seminar 34

Cultivating New Business: The BLENDS Model

LECTURETTE

Every business across the globe has one: It is that file cabinet stuffed full of inactive clients—some for legitimate reasons and many for reconcilable reasons!

Sales professionals should recognize the profitable potential of those inactive clients that no one wants to go after and that everyone knows are present. Realize that customers stop doing business with a vendor for basically one of (or a combination of) four basic reasons.

Customers Leave or Become Inactive Because:

1. **Financial Reason**—They think they can get a better buy somewhere else!

2. **Product or Service Needs Change**—They think you can't or know you can't meet their new needs!

3. **Perception**—They think that as a vendor you don't appreciate their level of business; they felt like a number on the roster of many clients, so they decide to leave.

4. **Communication Issues**—There have been miscommunications, negative communications, poor communication, lack of communication, or too much communication!

If you analyze a lost account from the perspective of these four basic reasons, it is very likely that you will be able to determine the reason why that client became inactive. If the client left for legitimate reasons, than move to the next one on the list. However, if that account became inactive for reconcilable reasons, go after that client with the BLENDS model.

Learn to recognize which approach would be most productive in engaging that inactive client and initiating a healthy new dialogue. Use the BLENDS Model for that added reconnection:

B—Directs you to contact an inactive account, which may require a lot of energy, especially immediately after you have had an interaction with an exceedingly positive client. Use that positive contact as an added **Boost** to reconnect with a lost account; your enthusiasm can be contagious!

L—Send that inactive account a **Letter** introducing yourself as a new point of contact and stating what you have to offer that could provide a better quality of life than the client presently enjoys. In this letter, share testimonials from current happy clients, and share collateral information, brochures, press clippings, and so on.

E—**Examine** the **Evidence** as to why the client was lost. Based upon those findings, determine how you could assist the client in today's marketplace with the products or services you now offer.

N—Offer to perform an account **Needs** Analysis for the client free of charge. Many new clients can be gained and many inactive clients can be regained if you partner with them and provide your expert analysis on how to proceed, what to produce, how to produce, or what to prepare for in today's market, free of charge!

D—Do Something for the client. Make contact, introduce yourself, and offer to do something for the client that only you can do and that would have value for them!

S—Provide the client with a current **Sample** of what you do that they may or may not be aware of and that is of value to the client.

Blending some activity in the area of account redevelopment into your typical daily activities is a great way to breathe life back into those dead accounts.

The odds are that within a few weeks of this mini-seminar, many sales professionals will have given up on this idea—but the true sales professionals will pace themselves and blend this account development work into their Sales Funnels (see Mini-Seminar 14) along with all their other account development activities.

ACTIVITY 34-A
CULTIVATING NEW BUSINESS: THE BLENDS MODEL

Identify three past active clients. For each client that you select, run the **BLENDS Model** checklist to determine how many action steps can be implemented. Then select the most powerful possibilities for that inactive client and implement them.

Client: _____

Best approach for this inactive client:

_____

(B—Identify the best parallel client that can be used as a reference or referral.)

_____

(L—Craft a letter to reintroduce your firm and you personally with an offer.)

_____

(E—Examine the evidence from the client history to determine why the client left.)

_____

(N—Perform a needs analysis for the client.)

_____

(D—Identify something of value that you can do for the client.)

_____

(S—Provide the client with a sample, service, or something that you have to offer.)

Client: _____

Best approach for this inactive client:

_____

(B—Identify the best parallel client that can be used as a reference or referral.)

_____

(L—Craft a letter to reintroduce your firm and you personally with an offer.)

_____

(E—Examine the evidence from the client history to determine why the client left.)

_____

(N—Perform a needs analysis for the client.)

_____

(D—Identify something of value that you can do for the client.)

_____

(S—Provide the client with a sample, service, or something that you have to offer.)

Client: _____

Best approach for this inactive client:

_____

(B—Identify the best parallel client that can be used as a reference or referral.)

_____

(L—Craft a letter to reintroduce your firm and you personally with an offer.)

_____

(E—Examine the evidence from the client history to determine why the client left.)

_____

(N—Perform a needs analysis for the client.)

_____

(D—Identify something of value that you can do for the client.)

_____

(S—Provide the client with a sample, service, or something that you have to offer.)

Copyright McGraw-Hill 2001. Original purchasers of this book are permitted to photocopy or customize this page by downloading it from www.books.mcgraw-hill.com/training/download. The document can then be opened, edited, and printed using Microsoft Word or other word processing software.

Mini-Seminar 35

Cross-Selling

Objective

1. To help participants look at every selling contact as an opportunity to cross-sell additional complementary products or services at the same time.

Time Required

20–30 minutes

Materials Needed

- A flip chart or whiteboard

- A list of core products or services offered by your organization or department

Directions for the Trainer

1. Read the lecturette prior to your training session, and take notes so you can use it as the basis for your own comments to the group.

2. Start the training session by summarizing the lecturette in your own words.

3. Activity 35-A: A cross-selling game: *First, take a stack of business cards* from every sales professional to be in the session, and label the reverse side of each card with a product or service you offer. Use enough cards for each sales professional so that you have a sizable working deck. *Second,* shuffle the deck and pass the cards around the room, having each participant take one card at a time. Let the deck go around the room several times until all the cards are drawn. *Third,* using the Five Step to Selling and focusing on the Presentation step (see Mini-Seminar 8), choose a participant at random and ask him to call out the sales professional's name on one of his cards and the labeled item on the reverse side. That sales professional will start the selling process,

using the Claim + Feature + Benefit + Naildown formula to sell the named item. *Fourth*, when that sales professional finishes, ask him to call out the name on one of the business cards he is holding and the item labeled on the back of it. That next sales professional continues the rapid fire series by communicating how his item can be associated (cross-sold) with the previous item.

Include all participants in at least one round. If time allows, go through the entire deck of cards. Make this a fun and engaging conversational activity. Some sales professionals may have to stretch to make a connection between the previous participant's presentation and theirs, and that's all right!

LECTURETTE

Cross-selling is the ability of a sales professional to meet a customer's immediate needs, while mentally evaluating other parallel products or services you represent to determine additional ways in which to meet the customer's needs.

Always be on the lookout for relevant cross-selling opportunities in each selling transaction. You should be able to evaluate what other offers you can make that will enhance, improve, and complement the current purchase at the same time you are closing that sale. A professional sales representative does this as a service to the buyer and not merely as a means of making another sale.

For example, if a man is buying a new tie, the sales professional might ask him if he has a tie tack. The customer may say no and may go on to say he doesn't like the look of a tie clasp. Cross-selling would then go into motion, with the sales professional saying something like this:

> "I can appreciate how you feel, I don't like them outwardly visible either. I wear a tie tack or tie clasp with all my ties, but as you can see, it's not visible. I wear the tie clasp under the tie and clip it against my inner tie and shirt to hold it in one place. The tie always stays perfectly aligned and no tie jewelry is visible."

This approach may convince the buyer to accept another product offering to complement the initial purchase.

Learn to recognize the appropriate cross-selling items among the products or services you offer, and role-play with your colleagues selling some of those products using the Claim + Feature + Benefit + Naildown sequence.

Every contact is an opportunity to meet the customer's needs. If you do a thorough job in the Inquiry stage of the selling process and uncover the customer's needs (immediate and future), then you can offer several options in the Presentation stage. Instead of saying, "You may need this," start the conversation by saying something like, "Along with this, you may also want to consider getting this and this."

The sales professional is always looking at the totality of needs that can be fulfilled by the range of products or services you represent, always with the best interest of the customer in mind.

If you are presenting the purchase of a skill development workshop to a prospect who accepts your offer, then you could potentially cross-sell books or audio tapes or CDs for the participants, as an after-workshop reinforcement of key content.

As a sales professional, you should always be thinking of additional opportunities within every transaction. The time of the initial transaction presents the best window of additional selling opportunity, although you can also cross-sell after the transaction. You can use a new product or service introduction as a reason to contact recent customers and let them know of the new offerings, pointing out how they might enhance the initial purchase.

Sales leaders fulfill their customers' needs completely by cross-selling all of the appropriate products or services offered by their organizations or departments.

Objective

1. To help participants look at every selling contact as an opportunity to up-sell the customer to a better or more profitable purchase, without jeopardizing the sales professional's or sales organization's integrity.

Time Required

15–20 minutes

Materials Needed

- A flip chart or whiteboard
- A list of core products or services offered by your organization or department

Directions for the Trainer

1. Read the lecturette prior to your training session, and take notes so you can use it as the basis for your own comments to the group.

2. Start the training session by summarizing the lecturette in your own words.

3. Activity 36-A: An up-selling game: *First, take a stack of business cards* from every sales professional to be in the session, and label the reverse side of each card with a product or service you offer. Use enough cards for each sales professional so that you have a sizable working deck. *Second,* shuffle the deck and pass the cards around the room, having each participant take one card at a time. Let the deck go around the room several times until all the cards are drawn. *Third,* using the Five Step to Selling and focusing on the Presentation step (see Mini-Seminar 8), choose a participant at random and ask her to call out the sales professional's name on one of her cards and the labeled item on the reverse side. That sales profes-

Mini-Seminar 36

Up-Selling

sional will start the selling process, using the Claim + Feature + Benefit + Nail-down formula to sell the named item. *Fourth,* when that sales professional finishes, ask her to call out the name on one of the business cards she is holding and the item labeled on the back of it. That next sales professional continues the rapid fire series by communicating how her item can be associated (up-sold) with the previous item.

Include all participants in at least one round. If time allows, go through the entire deck of cards. Make this a fun and engaging conversational activity. Some sales professionals may have to stretch to make a connection between the previous participant's presentation and theirs, and that's all right!

LECTURETTE

Up-selling is the ability of a sales professional to meet a customer's immediate needs, while mentally evaluating other parallel products or services you represent to determine if there are more efficient ways in which to meet the customer's needs.

Always be on the lookout for relevant up-selling opportunities in each selling transaction. You should be able to evaluate whether there is a better (special, new, improved, discontinued, rebated, more profitable) product or service that will enhance, improve, and complement the current purchase at the same time you are closing that sale. A professional sales representative does this as a service to the buyer and not merely as a means of making another sale.

> For example, if a man is buying a new suit, the sales professional might ask him how he plans to wear it. If the answer is for basic occasional wear, any suit might do. However, if the customer indicates that the suit will be worn often, in professional settings, then the sales professional has information that can be used to justify the purchase of a better, more expensive suit.

Learn to recognize the appropriate up-selling items among the products or services you offer, and role-play with your colleagues selling some of those products using the Claim + Feature + Benefit + Naildown sequence.

Every contact is an opportunity to meet the customer's needs. If you do a thorough job in the Inquiry stage of the selling process and uncover the customer's needs (immediate and future), then you can offer up-selling options in the Presentation stage. Instead of saying, "This will address your needs," start the conversation by saying something like, "You may want to consider this instead of that, because it will do a much better job at . . ."

The sales professional is always looking at the totality of needs that can be fulfilled by the range of products or services you represent, always with the best interest of the customer in mind.

If you are presenting the purchase of a motivational keynote speech for a conference to a prospect who accepts your offer, then you could potentially up-sell an additional breakout workshop while the speaker is there. You have now increased the transaction from one sale to two, with greater revenues and increased profitability.

As a sales professional, you should always be thinking of greater opportunities within every transaction. The time of the initial transaction presents the best window of up-selling opportunity, although you can also up-sell after the transaction. You can use a new product or service introduction as a reason to contact recent customers and let them know of the new offerings, pointing out how they might enhance the initial purchase.

Sales leaders fulfill their customers' needs completely by cross-selling all of the appropriate products or services offered by their organizations or departments.

Objective

1. To help participants look at every selling contact as an opportunity to build lasting and repeat business opportunities. Looking out for the customer's welfare might mean down-selling to better and/or more efficiently serve the customer's needs.

Time Required

15–20 minutes

Materials Needed

- A flip chart or whiteboard

- A list of core products or services offered by your organization or department

Directions for the Trainer

1. Read the lecturette prior to your training session, and take notes so you can use it as the basis for your own comments to the group.

2. Start the training session by summarizing the lecturette in your own words.

3. Activity 37-A: A down-selling game: *First, take a stack of business cards* from every sales professional to be in the session, and label the reverse side of each card with a product or service you offer. Use enough cards for each sales professional so that you have a sizable working deck. *Second,* shuffle the deck and pass the cards around the room, having each participant take one card at a time. Let the deck go around the room several times until all the cards are drawn. *Third,* using the Five Step to Selling and focusing on the Presentation step (see Mini-Seminar 8), choose a participant at random and ask him to call out the sales professional's name on one of

Mini-Seminar 37

Down-Selling to Better Serve the Client

his cards and the labeled item on the reverse side. That sales professional will start the selling process, using the Claim + Feature + Benefit + Naildown formula to sell the named item. *Fourth,* when that sales professional finishes, ask any participant who is holding a card with a viable down-selling product or service listed on it to call out the name of the sales professional listed on the front of that card. Then that sales professional continues the rapid fire series by communicating how his item can be associated (down-sold) with the previous item, and why it might be a better purchase for the customer.

Include all participants in at least one round. If time allows, go through the entire deck of cards. Make this a fun and engaging conversational activity. Some sales professionals may have to stretch to make a connection between the previous participant's presentation and theirs, and that's all right!

LECTURETTE

Down-selling is the ability of a sales professional to meet a customer's immediate needs, while mentally evaluating other parallel products or services you represent to determine if there are more efficient ways in which to meet the customer's needs.

Always be on the lookout for relevant down-selling opportunities in each selling transaction. You should be able to evaluate down-selling offers you can make of a better (special, new, improved, discontinued, rebated, more cost-effective) product or service that will serve the client's needs more appropriately.

For example, suppose a person enters an electronics shop to buy an appliance or entertainment system and is looking at the high-end product. If the sales professional determines through dialogue that a similar unit at a lower price would address the customer's needs, you might want to avoid making the high-end sale. By allowing the buyer to make an informed decision between the two purchases, you do a service to the client and also provide a significant reason for the client to do more business with you in the future.

Learn to recognize the appropriate down-selling items among the products or services you offer, and role-play with your colleagues selling some of those products using the Claim + Feature + Benefit + Naildown sequence.

Every contact is an opportunity to meet the customer's needs. If you do a thorough job in the Inquiry stage of the selling process and uncover the customer's needs (immediate and future), then you can offer appropriate down-selling options in the Presentation stage. Instead of saying, "This will address your needs," start the conversation by saying something like, "You may want to consider this instead of that, because this will do the job you require and also save you some money."

The sales professional is always looking at the totality of needs that can be fulfilled by the range of products or services you represent, always with the best interest of the customer in mind.

Suppose you were presenting the purchase of a full-day educational workshop to a prospect, and you determined that you could satisfactorily deliver what the customer needs in a half-day session, thereby saving the client money. If you make that recommendation, you may find that you have gained a client for life!

As a sales professional, you should always be thinking of additional opportunities within every transaction. The time of the initial transaction presents the best window of down-selling opportunity.

Sales leaders fulfilling their customers' needs completely by cross-selling all of the appropriate products or services offered by their organizations or departments.

Mini-Seminar 38

Identifying Your Target-Rich Environment (TRE)

Objective

1. To help participants streamline their prospecting efforts and put their Sales Funnel contact activity on a fast track.

Time Required

15–20 minutes

Materials Needed

- One copy of each of the two activity sheets for each participant

- A flip chart or whiteboard

Directions for the Trainer

1. Read the lecturette prior to your training session, and take notes so you can use it as the basis for your own comments to the group.

2. Start the training session by summarizing the lecturette in your own words; then pass out the activity sheets.

3. Activity Sheet 38-A: Have participants identify their top ten customers and then review the names to determine whether there are any patterns among the sources of clients (environments, demographics, organizations, industries, etc.). Debrief by asking how many common areas were identified per participant.

4. Activity 38-B: Then have each participant pair off with another colleague and brainstorm all the other vertical (other industries, geographies, etc.) and horizontal (same industries, geographies, etc.) markets where like Qualified Prospects could be found.

LECTURETTE

Great sales professionals realize that the 80/20 Rule (see Mini-Seminar 15) applies to selling—a larger percentage (80 percent) of ones' business comes from a smaller portion (20 percent) of the contact base you maintain. The markets or areas from which you tend to draw the majority of your business is known as your Target Rich Environment (TRE).

To increase sales effectiveness, you identify this area that seems to generate greater business opportunities—your TRE!

Many sales professionals don't recognize that they tend to focus their activities in specific directions or sell into specific areas. One way to increase your awareness of a tendency to focus on specific areas is to identify the Standard Industry Code number (SIC) for the buyers that tend to generate the bulk of your activity. By identifying the businesses, associations, or companies responsible for the largest percentage of your business by their respective SIC numbers, you can then reference other like Target Rich Environments with the same SIC number. Then you can ensure that you are thoroughly working your TRE every day, becoming widely known as the expert person within that TRE.

For example, if you tend to realize more business from the pharmaceutical industry, then explore every means by which you can identify pharmaceutical businesses and even pharmaceutical-related businesses to contact. You can target only well-known businesses within your area, or target a geographical region in which to work.

Once you know that you are actively, consistently, and thoroughly engaging your primary TRE, then you can focus efforts on other suspects and prospects in complementary TREs who would also be likely customers.

ACTIVITY 38-A
IDENTIFYING YOUR TARGET-RICH ENVIRONMENT (TRE)

List your top ten customers (the clients who are at the bottom of your Sales Funnel). Then review the names to determine if there is a pattern of several clients having anything in common—identify a possible TRE.

1. _____

2. _____

3. _____

4. _____

5. _____

6. _____

7. _____

8. _____

9. _____

10. _____

Copyright McGraw-Hill 2001. Original purchasers of this book are permitted to photocopy or customize this page by downloading it from www.books.mcgraw-hill.com/training/download. The document can then be opened, edited, and printed using Microsoft Word or other word processing software.

ACTIVITY 38-B
IDENTIFYING YOUR TARGET-RICH ENVIRONMENT (TRE)

PARTICIPANT'S
HANDOUT

Pair off with a colleague and review each other's lists from Activity Sheet 38-A. Brainstorm together other TREs for both of your combined active clients to see how many TREs you can come up with.

Copyright McGraw-Hill 2001. Original purchasers of this book are permitted to photocopy or customize this page by downloading it from www.books.mcgraw-hill.com/training/download. The document can then be opened, edited, and printed using Microsoft Word or other word processing software.

Mini-Seminar 39

Cultivating Other TREs

Objective

1. To help participants streamline their prospecting efforts and put their Sales Funnel contact activity on a fast track by quickly identifying other market-rich environments to work in.

Time Required

15–20 minutes

Materials Needed

- One copy of each of the two activity sheets for each participant

- A flip chart or whiteboard

Directions for the Trainer

1. Read the lecturette prior to your training session, and take notes so you can use it as the basis for your own comments to the group.

2. Start the training session by summarizing the lecturette in your own words; then pass out the activity sheets.

3. Activity 39-A: Have participants identify their top ten customers and then review the names to determine whether there are any patterns among the sources of clients (environments, demographics, organizations, industries, etc.). Debrief by asking how many common areas were identified per participant.

4. Activity 39-B: Then have each participant pair off with another colleague and brainstorm all the other vertical (other industries, geographies, etc.) and horizontal (same industries, geographies, etc.) markets where like Qualified Prospects could be found.

LECTURETTE

Great sales professionals understand that taking care of their primary market is critical to selling success. Along with this activity, there is also a need to be continually cultivating new future business.

The 80/20 Rule (see Mini-Seminar 15) applies to selling—a larger percentage (80 percent) of one's business comes from a smaller portion (20 percent) of the contact base you maintain. Learn to recognize the markets or areas from which you tend to derive the majority of your business. This is known as your Target Rich Environment (TRE).

While sales professionals are actively taking care of the primary TRE, there is always a need to be planting seeds of contact for future orders or harvesting the seeds of past successful sales.

To determine where the best future markets may be, start by analyzing the core product or services you offer and seek to determine where there might be additional viable markets to cultivate.

Example: If you offer a product or service that you tend to sell to high school students, your primary TRE would be a physical high school complex. Additional TREs could be identified by determining where else one could attain the names of high school age customers for contact.

The seeds of other or new TREs that you might concentrate your energies on daily might be:

1. shopping malls,

2. sports complexes or gyms,

3. church youth groups,

4. sports teams or coaches,

5. YMCAs,

6. Boys' and Girls' Clubs,

7. honor roll listings in local newspapers,

8. yearbook listings, and

9. driver's license register rolls.

After identifying the products or services you have to offer and the related customer who most typically buys, you must also be working to identify other sources of buyers for your offerings. An easy way to accomplish this is to look for all other viable markets for your product or service, and start becoming known within those markets.

You can do this by looking at business buying patterns within your own industry, by looking at where your colleagues tend to do more of their business, or by identifying all potential buyers in the same industry (horizontal) you presently sell to the most. You can also identify potentially lucrative markets by reviewing the actual product or service and exploring who in other markets or other TREs might be receptive to your offering.

ACTIVITY 39-A
CULTIVATING OTHER TREs

List your top ten customers (the clients who are at the bottom of your Sales Funnel). Then review the names to determine if there is a pattern of several clients having anything in common—identify a possible TRE.

1. _____

2. _____

3. _____

4. _____

5. _____

6. _____

7. _____

8. _____

9. _____

10. _____

Copyright McGraw-Hill 2001. Original purchasers of this book are permitted to photocopy or customize this page by downloading it from www.books.mcgraw-hill.com/training/download. The document can then be opened, edited, and printed using Microsoft Word or other word processing software.

ACTIVITY 39-B
CULTIVATING OTHER TREs

Pair off with a colleague and review each other's lists from Activity Sheet 38-A. Brainstorm together other TREs for both of your combined active clients to see how many TREs you can come up with.

Copyright McGraw-Hill 2001. Original purchasers of this book are permitted to photocopy or customize this page by downloading it from www.books.mcgraw-hill.com/training/download. The document can then be opened, edited, and printed using Microsoft Word or other word processing software.

Objectives

1. To help participants identify the two dominant reasons why a customer may be purchasing from you and the two dominant reasons why customers leave.

2. To help participants understand two powerful ways to measure the level of service being provided in any selling transaction, and how to sell against a competitor based upon these two factors.

Time Required

20–30 minutes

Materials Needed

- One copy of the activity sheet for each participant

- A flip chart or whiteboard

Directions for the Trainer

1. Read the lecturette prior to your training session, and take notes so you can use it as the basis for your own comments to the group.

2. Start the training session by summarizing the lecturette in your own words; then pass out copies of the activity sheet.

3. Activity 40-A: Have participants identify the last customer they know of losing, and measure the reasons on the CSI chart. Then discuss ways they could have prevented that from happening. Also, brainstorm ways to sell against that deficiency to get the lost customers back. Debrief by asking some participants to share examples with the group.

Mini-Seminar 40

Why Customers Love You or Leave You

4. Activity 40-B: Have participants form teams of 2 to 3. Post the CSI diagram on a wall. With a roll of tape, make a sticky ball for each team. Then have teams compete at CSI Tape Darts: Each team throws its tape ball at the chart; the quadrant the tape ball lands in is the one the team must represent in a sales Presentation. Have each team give a sales Presentation designed to sell against any inherent negatives and keep their prospect or customer.

LECTURETTE

Many selling organizations believe that they have customers in large part because of the great service they offer and/or the exclusive selling rights for a product or service within a particular market. Many times this may be true; but a sales professional's understanding of how your organization measures up on an objective **Customer Service Index (CSI)** may reveal the real reasons why a customer does business with you and why that same customer may leave.

Building customer loyalty today is an extremely difficult task. Providing a customer with Excellent customer care may actually be the impetus for a customer to leave, if that customer expects Exceptional customer care. To ensure that a customer gained is a customer kept, sales professionals and internal customer care agents must continuously strive to provide Exceptional customer care.

To understand the CSI, recognize that customers measure two basic variables delivered by an organization they purchase from: the product or service itself, and the people they deal with at the selling company. Both variables are measured on a scale of low to high. The customer's buying or repeat buying decisions are based upon the measures for these two variables. These two variables also directly influence a buyer's loyalty, or lack of loyalty.

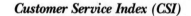

Customer Service Index (CSI)

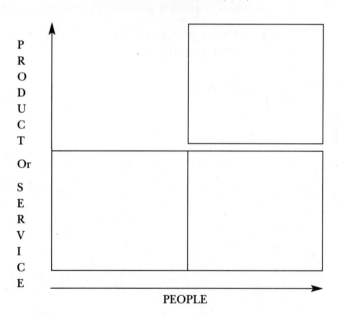

In using the CSI diagram, measure how a customer might rate the actual product or service being purchased on the vertical axis, from low at the bottom to progressively higher as one moves up the scale. Then customers measure the way the people associated with the transaction handled that encounter, from poor or low to the left and progressively better further to the right on the scale.

To label the four differing quadrants, a CSI score in the bottom left quadrant would be labeled Poor customer care and would obviously lead to lost business.

A score in the bottom right quadrant would be labeled Excellent customer care. Although the product or service the customer bought didn't meet or exceed expectations, the sales professional represented the business well and in essence carried the organization.

A score in the top left quadrant would also be labeled Excellent customer care. Again, this is a very misleading label, and the sales professional should understand that business is taking place here in large part because of product loyalty or brand loyalty, but not because the sales professional is delivering great care. This situation can lead to future lost business.

The ultimate goal of every sales professional is to have a CSI score in the top right quadrant. This indicates that the product or service and the sales professional both exceeded the customer's expectations. This quadrant is labeled Exceptional customer care!

From an organizational standpoint, sales professionals should recognize that customers who score in bottom right quadrant will leave when their relationship with a sales professional ends. The same is true for customers who score in the top left quadrant; as soon as another vendor enters your market with an equal product or service, the customers will leave in droves; they are frustrated with giving their money and business to an organization in which they feel the sales professionals and customer service representatives don't appreciate them.

A sales professional must always strive for business transactions to score in the top right quadrant of the CSI scale.

ACTIVITY 40-A
WHY CUSTOMERS LOVE YOU OR LEAVE YOU

Last Customer Departure: _____

Why Did the Customer Leave? _____

_____

_____

What Could Have Been Done to Retain the Customer? _____

_____

_____

_____

_____

Copyright McGraw-Hill 2001. Original purchasers of this book are permitted to photocopy or customize this page by downloading it from www.books.mcgraw-hill.com/training/download. The document can then be opened, edited, and printed using Microsoft Word or other word processing software.

Objectives

1. To have participants recognize the impact of customer relationships on sales effectiveness.

2. To teach participants how customers measure their relationships with salespersons and organizations.

Time Required

15–20 minutes

Materials Needed

- One copy of each of the four activity sheets for each participant

- A flip chart or whiteboard

Directions for the Trainer

1. Read the lecturette prior to your training session, and take notes so you can use it as the basis for your own comments to the group.

2. Start the training session by summarizing the lecturette in your own words; then pass out the activity sheets.

3. Activity Sheet 41-A: Discuss times when the participants have been customers recently and were made to feel that the vendor was delivering Reliable C.A.R.E. service and how that affected their purchase decisions.

4. Activity Sheet 41-B: Discuss times when the participants have been customers and were made to feel that the vendor did not deliver Reliable C.A.R.E. service. For each example, discuss ways in which the vendor could have turned the experience into a positive one. Help participants to recognize how easy that often is.

Mini-Seminar 41

Building Lasting Sales Relationships by Providing Reliable C.A.R.E.

5. Activity Sheet 41-C: Discuss how participants can deliver Reliable C.A.R.E. to every prospect or customer. Have them share their examples for each letter category of the formula. Point out similar ideas and approaches as well as the different ideas that come from the group. Have participants write action plans for delivering each category of C.A.R.E.

6. Activity Sheet 41-D: Discuss how all of the sales professionals in the organization can strive to ensure that the organization delivers Reliable C.A.R.E. What can the organization do to complement sales professionals' individual efforts?

LECTURETTE

Building customer loyalty is essential to effective long-term selling. Studies repeatedly illustrate that it takes more time, money, and energy to gain one new customer than it does to keep an existing customer.

Customers want to do business with credible vendors. Your credibility is the customer's perception of your ability to meet or exceed expectations in five categories:

1. Reliable—How reliable are you and what you represent? Do you deliver what you say you will? Do you do what you say you will? Do you produce what's expected?

2. Caring—Do customers feel that you genuinely care for them, appreciate them, respect them, and have their best interests in mind?

3. Attractive—Are you and your organization an attractive option as compared to others in the market place? Do you meet or exceed the initial expectations of the customer?

4. Responsive—Do clients feel that you address their needs in a timely manner? Do you deliver and follow up in a time frame that is at or ahead of expectations?

5. Empathetic—Do customers feel that you understand and acknowledge their positions or views?

In a 1997 survey of 10,059 respondents, these were qualities that customers said they looked for in a vendor. The top response was "appreciation," which is another way of stating "care for the customer." How do you score yourself against each letter category? Are you earning an A+?

This model is called the Reliable C.A.R.E. formula. Measure yourself personally against this model, and then measure the others in your organization who deal with your customers (other sales professionals, customer service coordinators, billing representatives, receptionists). But until you pass all five categories, don't talk to your colleagues about their shortcomings. In today's fast-paced, highly competitive marketplace, your credibility can be your greatest advantage. Do you truly provide customers with Reliable C.A.R.E.?

ACTIVITY SHEET 41-A
RELIABLE C.A.R.E. EXPERIENCE INVENTORY

PARTICIPANT'S HANDOUT

Reflect on an experience you had recently when you were the customer, and the level of service you received met or surpassed your expectations in the categories of the **Reliable C.A.R.E.** formula. Identify what specific actions were taken by that sales professional or customer service representative in delivering the product or service you were purchasing.

Vendor: _____

What You Were Buying: _____

Which categories did the salesperson meet, and how?

R: Reliable _____

_____

_____

C: Caring _____

_____

_____

A: Attractive _____

_____

_____

R: Responsive _____

_____

_____

E: Empathetic _____

_____

_____

Copyright McGraw-Hill 2001. Original purchasers of this book are permitted to photocopy or customize this page by downloading it from www.books.mcgraw-hill.com/training/download. The document can then be opened, edited, and printed using Microsoft Word or other word processing software.

ACTIVITY SHEET 41-B
RELIABLE C.A.R.E. EXPERIENCE INVENTORY

Reflect on an experience you had recently when you were the customer, and the level of service you received did not meet your expectations in the categories of the **Reliable C.A.R.E.** formula. Identify what specific disappointing actions were taken by that sales professional or customer service representative in delivering the product or service you were purchasing. Then identify ways in which that negative experience could have been turned into a positive selling opportunity.

Vendor: _____

What You Were Buying: _____

Which categories did the salesperson *fail* to deliver and why? *How could the salesperson* have met each one?

R: Reliable _____

_____

_____

C: Caring _____

_____

_____

A: Attractive _____

_____

_____

R: Responsive _____

_____

_____

E: Empathetic _____

_____

_____

Copyright McGraw-Hill 2001. Original purchasers of this book are permitted to photocopy or customize this page by downloading it from www.books.mcgraw-hill.com/training/download. The document can then be opened, edited, and printed using Microsoft Word or other word processing software.

ACTIVITY SHEET 41-C
RELIABLE C.A.R.E. SELF-DELIVERY INVENTORY

Analyze your present sales abilities and how you interact with individuals, whether face-to-face, within group situations, over the telephone, via e-mail, or in any other interaction. Think about how you can always meet or exceed the expectations of others in each of the **Reliable C.A.R.E.** formula categories.

Which categories do you easily meet, and how? Which categories do you need to work on?

R: Reliable   _____
                _____
                _____
                _____

C: Caring   _____
                _____
                _____
                _____

A: Attractive   _____
                _____
                _____
                _____

R: Responsive   _____
                _____
                _____
                _____

E: Empathetic   _____
                _____
                _____
                _____

Copyright McGraw-Hill 2001. Original purchasers of this book are permitted to photocopy or customize this page by downloading it from www.books.mcgraw-hill.com/training/download. The document can then be opened, edited, and printed using Microsoft Word or other word processing software.

ACTIVITY SHEET 41-D
RELIABLE C.A.R.E. ORGANIZATIONAL
DELIVERY INVENTORY

PARTICIPANT'S
HANDOUT

Analyze your organization and how everyone interacts with individuals, whether face-to-face, within group situations, over the telephone, via e-mail, or in any other interaction. Think about how the organization can always meet or exceed the expectations of others in each of the **Reliable C.A.R.E.** formula categories.

Which categories can you easily meet, and how? Which categories need work?

R: Reliable   _____

_____

_____

_____

C: Caring   _____

_____

_____

_____

A: Attractive   _____

_____

_____

_____

R: Responsive   _____

_____

_____

_____

E: Empathetic   _____

_____

_____

_____

Copyright McGraw-Hill 2001. Original purchasers of this book are permitted to photocopy or customize this page by downloading it from www.books.mcgraw-hill.com/training/download. The document can then be opened, edited, and printed using Microsoft Word or other word processing software.

Objectives

1. To impress upon participants the importance of following up with prospects and clients.

2. To illustrate three powerful ways to leave a lasting positive impression in a customer's mind.

Time Required

15–20 minutes

Materials Needed

- Small pieces of paper, each labeled with the letter V, A, or K—an equal number with each letter

- A flip chart or whiteboard

Directions for the Trainer

1. Read the lecturette prior to your training session, and take notes so you can use it as the basis for your own comments to the group.

2. Start the training session by summarizing the lecturette in your own words; then pass out the pieces of paper.

3. Have participants identify as many ways as they can to follow up with a prospect or customer, using the lettered category on the pieces of paper they received. Then have them partner with a colleague to share ideas. Debrief with the whole group by soliciting ideas for each letter from the teams to develop a combined list of follow-up options on a whiteboard or flip chart. Copy this master list and give copies to everyone after the session for their future use.

Mini-Seminar 42

Three Keys to Follow-Up Success

LECTURETTE

Remember: The early bird catches the worm, or so goes the saying! The same is true of the sales professional who does the best professional follow-up.

The opportunity to make a sale is a special event. When a prospect requests more information or a customer has just bought your offer, the window of opportunity to capitalize upon that activity is small.

Studies indicate that follow-up alone can significantly increase a sales professional's closing ratio and business volume. Studies also reveal that most sales professionals don't take advantage of the opportunity for additional relationship building and potential increased sales by following up!

There are three ways in which a sales professional can follow up with customers. Depending upon the channel of follow-up selected, specific options become evident. The three channels are:

1. visual,

2. auditory, and

3. kinesthetic (interactive or face-to-face).

There are a lot of ways to keep your name and message in front of prospects and customers to maintain your name presence with them. Here are some of the specific action items for each channel of follow-up:

Visual

1. Send a personal note or a card with your name on it.

2. Send an e-mail message.

3. Fax a follow-up note, reminder, or FYI message.

4. Send a special thank-you gift or offering.

5. Forward an article or clipping of relevant interest.

Auditory

1. Leave a personal voice mail message.

2. Make a follow-up telephone call.

3. Send a recorded gift offering.

Kinesthetic

1. Make a personal follow-up visit.

2. Send an invitation to an event or pre-event.

3. Have a field representative make a personal follow-up visit.

Remember that for any action to have maximum impact, it must be done in a timely manner and the action must be relevant for that prospect or customer. The timing of follow-up is particularly critical. Done too soon, it may appear overbearing; done too late, it may seem like an afterthought.

Remember: The early sales professional gets the sale and gets the repeat sale!

Objective

1. To show participants how to become known as an acknowledged expert in their sales area.

Time Required

20–30 minutes

Materials Needed

- Paper cutouts of logos, or sample products with notable logos on them (Examples: McDonald's, Xerox, Kleenex, Taco Bell, IBM, Kodak, Motorola)

- A flip chart or whiteboard

Directions for the Trainer

1. Read the lecturette prior to your training session, and take notes so you can use it as the basis for your own comments to the group.

2. Start the training session by summarizing the lecturette in your own words.

3. Have participants work in teams to identify what things each company does to establish its market leadership. How do successful companies position with their respective brands to achieve brand recognition? Then have participants identify ways to differentiate themselves in the marketplace and establish their own brand recognition.

Mini-Seminar 43

Building Your Brand Recognition

LECTURETTE

Establishing brand recognition takes hard, consistent, and continuous work. Sales professionals can differentiate themselves from others in the marketplace by establishing what their products, their services, and they themselves are known for.

Businesses invest millions of dollars to establish brand recognition and build brand loyalty. When you see the golden arches of McDonald's, you automatically think, "fast, inexpensive food" and more specifically, "sandwich foods like hamburgers, fish, and chicken and the famous french fries." When you see the yellow Kodak box, you immediately think of "quality film for taking pictures."

For practically every major business name or logo, the consumer's mind has been conditioned to expect certain brands and goods.

Recognize what the differentiator is for your organization and for you individually. Then work relentlessly to deliver that message with everything you do.

Sales professionals can develop brand recognition and send that continuous message to their respective markets by their daily strategic marketing and selling efforts. Review Mini-Seminar 1 and the Position Statement you developed—remember that in part, the statement said, "This is who I am and what I am all about in the selling world!"

With this clarity of purpose in mind, guide your involvement, commitments, and volunteer activities in a corresponding direction. For example, if you want to be known as the person to come to for services or products connected to high-end widgets, then participate in conferences that attract prospects for those widgets. Offer to contribute articles to journals, newsletters, or websites for users of those widgets.

Mini-Seminar 44

Using Your Business Card As Your Number 1 Selling Instrument

Objectives

1. To impress upon participants the importance of always having business cards with them.

2. To help participants recognize ways to use their business cards in the selling process for impact and success.

Time Required

15–20 minutes

Materials Needed

- Bring one copy of each participant's business card to the session, in case any participants don't have cards with them. *Do not preannounce the need for business cards for this session.*

- If appropriate, bring a new box of 500 business cards for each sales professional to this meeting, to be given to them as a seven-day assignment.

- A flip chart or whiteboard

Directions for the Trainer

1. Read the lecturette prior to your training session, and take notes so you can use it as the basis for your own comments to the group.

2. Start the training session by asking the group how many of them have business cards with them at the present time. Ask those who do to place one business card in front of them for later use. If any participants don't have cards, ask them to borrow one from a colleague. Then summarize the lecturette in your own words.

3. Activity 44-A: Have participants brainstorm all the smart ways that sales professionals can use their business cards as selling instruments

in the next week. Also discuss all the places where they should have their business cards stored for easy access and use. Then develop a list of as many ways as possible to get their business cards into the hands of targeted prospects and suspects. Make it a sales professional's game to move 500 cards into the Suspect, Prospect, or Customer levels of the Sales Funnel in the next week.

Have each sales professional write on the reverse of a business card an action plan for all the people they intend to contact in the next week. Then have them either copy that onto a second card or make a photocopy; let participants trade the copies with another sales professional who will act as an accountability coach. Have partners work with one another in the next week to ensure greater commitment to the action plans.

LECTURETTE

Great sales professionals don't miss a selling opportunity, nor do they miss an opportunity to network with others and place their personal business cards into others' hands.

The business card is to a sales professional what the road sign is along the highways of life; it tells people who you are and how to reach you. Successful sales professionals know that a great selling opportunity may present itself at any time. Having a business card to offer to someone can differentiate a super sales professional from an ordinary salesperson within a pack.

Business cards also provide a powerful means of measuring whether a sales professional is investing enough time with Suspects and Prospects in the Sales Funnel (Mini-Seminar 14). Each contact with a Suspect or Prospect is an opportunity to offer your card. If you are in a sales position, getting your cards into the right hands is critical. Don't warehouse your business cards in your desk drawer. Savvy sales managers use the number of business cards a sales professional orders to determine who is and who is not prospecting, marketing, networking, and selling!

A business card can be used in many ways to bring greater value to the recipient and yield greater returns for the sales professional.

1. As most business cards are blank on the reverse side, this is a great place to make specific notations for the prospect or customer about special Features or Benefits you are offering. People are more inclined to keep your business card, and more inclined to discard the brochures and handouts that sales professionals tend to load them down with.

   A powerful way to use the business card as a customized selling brochure is to draw a small circle on the blank side—about the size of a small coin. Inside the circle, write a word or a few words, concentrating on the key point you want the receiver to remember about your offer or Presentation. Then, for any key offer, price, feature, or benefit that relates to the encircled notation, draw short axis lines outward from the circle and write a simple notation on each line. Visually, a wheel with spokes appears, with key words that mean something to the recipient of the card. You have given the customer a special, customized reference instrument.

2. Use your business card as a means of soliciting someone's name and title by offering your card to the other person at the beginning of the sales conversation and requesting hers. Then take her card and leave it in front of you during your sales conversation or Presentation, as a reminder to use the other person's name.

3. Offer an extra card to any prospect who becomes a happy customer, as a means of recruiting a referral agent. Say, for example: "Here's an extra card for you, should you know of someone who would benefit from this product or service as you have. Thank you."

4. In any follow-up letters, thank-you letters, or prospecting letters (Rule 1/12/50, Mini-Seminar 31), always include a few cards—one for the intended reader, and extras for the customer to pass along to others.

5. Place your business cards in giveaway drawing bowls or jars on counters in stores with a high volume of traffic among your profile prospects and customers. Place the card in such a way that it is held within that bowl or jar as a billboard for viewers.

6. Look for display areas where your business card can be tacked up, included in other merchant's direct mail circulars or envelopes or mail packs, magnetized and hung up, or used as a bookmark.

There are lots of powerful ways to utilize your business cards as powerful selling instruments. The cards sent out are like seeds. The more seeds you plant, the greater your potential harvest!

Objective

1. To help participants understand their marketability, given their relationship to the competition.

Time Required

20–30 minutes

Materials Needed

- One copy of the activity sheet for each participant

- A flip chart or whiteboard

Directions for the Trainer

1. Read the lecturette prior to your training session, and take notes so you can use it as the basis for your own comments to the group.

2. Start the training session by summarizing the lecturette in your own words; then pass out the activity sheets.

3. Activity Sheet 45-A: Have participants identify major competitors, either by specific threat, by key products or services they offer, or by industry position overall. Then have them work in teams to complete a generalized competitive analysis form and discuss how to position themselves against competitors.

Mini-Seminar 45

Competitive Analysis: You Versus ?

LECTURETTE

Everyone has competition in some form and to some degree. A sales professional knows who those competitive challengers are and has well-defined plans for selling against them in interactions with prospects and active clients.

Embrace the challenge of competition rather than fearing it. Learn how to professionally and confidently address competitive challenges and threats as you present yourself to customers and how to compensate for any weakness in your offer.

One powerful way to objectively compare and contrast any specific product, service, or organization in comparison to any primary competitor is to use a Ben Franklin Analysis Model. Legend has it that whenever Benjamin Franklin needed to make a decision, he would take a piece of paper, divide it into equal columns, and place at the top of each column the different issues he was perplexed over. He would then proceed to chronicle all of the positives for each issue under the appropriate header. When he was done, he would make his choice based on whichever column had more responses.

This same model can be used to compare and contrast products, services, or organizational threats to a sales professional's lineup. For example, you could use the Ben Franklin Analysis Model to compare strengths between your organization and your number one competitor overall.

Our Organization	Primary Competitor: _____

Successful sales professionals have the ability to look objectively at what they represent and what the competition has to offer. In fact, the more product knowledge a sales professional has about the competition, the more effective he or she can become at focusing prospecting efforts, honing selling Presentation skills, and qualifying Suspects as potential customers.

When you think in terms of competitive analysis and reflect upon your strengths and weaknesses as compared to a competitor, you can make informed decisions. Think of a professional sporting team coach on game day. It would be reasonable to expect that the coach would know by name the opposing team's coach and primary players. The coach would have studied the strengths and weaknesses of the other team and coached his players on what to expect from the opposing team. The competitive analysis affects sales professionals' decisions and choices for positioning themselves for success.

ACTIVITY SHEET 45-A
BEN FRANKLIN ANALYSIS

Complete this Ben Franklin Analysis for an organizational comparison, product comparison, or service comparison. Then discuss ways to sell over any differences noted.

Category: _____   _____
Strengths or Weaknesses   Strengths or Weaknesses

Copyright McGraw-Hill 2001. Original purchasers of this book are permitted to photocopy or customize this page by downloading it from www.books.mcgraw-hill.com/training/download. The document can then be opened, edited, and printed using Microsoft Word or other word processing software.

Objective

1. To teach participants how to identify potential Advocates and how to nurture those relationships.

Time Required

20–30 minutes

Materials Needed

- A list of each participant's most active clients and longest-tenured clients

- One copy of the activity sheet for each participant

- A flip chart or whiteboard

Directions for the Trainer

1. Read the lecturette prior to your training session, and take notes so you can use it as the basis for your own comments to the group.

2. Start the training session by asking the group how many of them have clients who have ever sent or are currently sending them business leads. Then summarize the lecturette in your own words.

3. Activity 46-A: Have participants identify their top clients (based on dollar volume, longest tenure, loyalty, etc.) and determine which ones, if any, have ever sent them business. Discuss what may have precipitated that action and how that can be replicated in the future.

Mini-Seminar 46

Cultivating Advocates from Existing Clients

LECTURETTE

Great sales professionals don't miss a selling opportunity, nor do they miss an opportunity to network with others to find ways to make others' lives better and easier. By doing so, they cultivate powerful relationships.

Examine your professional and personal life to identify individuals who believe so powerfully in you that they don't hesitate to talk you up to others. These people can serve as a valuable component in your selling plan.

These people who believe so powerfully in you can be your Advocates—sending business to you, and recommending you as the solution provider for others' challenges and problems. These are the individuals who promote you when you are not around to promote yourself.

Advocates are people you turn to for advice, suggestions, and counsel. You can bounce marketing and selling ideas off them. You can turn to them when you have a new product or service available and you want to get the word out. They are well-positioned in the marketplace themselves and know people who respect them and who you can cultivate for immediate and future business opportunities.

Advocates believe strongly in you, both personally and professionally. Therefore, they can serve as never-ending sources of qualified contacts for your Sales Funnel.

Search for Advocates among your most loyal customers, your largest-volume customers, and prospects who sing your praises but for legitimate reasons have not yet become active clients. Look inward to your organization and outward to your social or personal contacts for people who respect you, admire you, and look up to you. Look for decision makers in industry, associations, clubs, social organizations, church, and so on—wherever you engage others and where there may be opportunities for both sides to gain from one another.

Advocates are everywhere. Successful sales professionals cultivate them, appreciate them, and thank them for being active participants in their selling effectiveness.

ACTIVITY 46-A
CULTIVATING ADVOCATES FROM EXISTING CLIENTS

Advocate candidates for my selling success are:

Contact

**How Likely Are They to
Advocate You to Others? (Y or N)**

1. Oldest client: _____ _____ _____

2. Newest client: _____ _____ _____

3. Most $ client: _____ _____ _____

4. Others: _____ _____

5. Others: _____ _____

6. Others: _____ _____

7. Others: _____ _____

8. Others: _____ _____

9. Others: _____ _____

10. Others: _____ _____

Now go back and check off the names of those contacts who you know have sent you contacts in the past. These are potential candidates for you to consider courting as Advocates to help you grow and establish your business.

Copyright McGraw-Hill 2001. Original purchasers of this book are permitted to photocopy or customize this page by downloading it from www.books.mcgraw-hill.com/training/download. The document can then be opened, edited, and printed using Microsoft Word or other word processing software.

Mini-Seminar 47

Mastering the Telephone

Objectives

1. To help participants recognize that the telephone is a powerful contact instrument if used effectively.

2. To help participants learn ways to break indifference and procrastination barriers, overcome phone resistance, leave motivating messages, manage the phone conversation, and identify the best and worst times for making phone calls.

Time Required

20–30 minutes

Materials Needed

- An office phone with corded handset, a headset, a cell phone, a clock, and a weekly calendar (desk blotter calendar, day planner, etc.)

- A flip chart or whiteboard

Directions for the Trainer

1. Read the lecturette prior to your training session, and take notes so you can use it as the basis for your own comments to the group.

2. Start the training session by summarizing the lecturette in your own words.

3. Activity 47-A: Call several of the participants' voice mail systems to hear typical recorded voice mail messages, and review typical messages left by sales professionals in someone else's voice mail receiving system. Discuss with the group how those messages could be tailored to make them more energized, motivational, and action-oriented. Discuss more effective ways to leave messages and get messages, ways to energize outbound calls, and ways to overcome procrastination.

LECTURETTE

The number of contacts that can be made via the telephone as compared to face-to-face contacts is significantly greater. Successful sales professionals recognize that the telephone is a tool for sales success.

Most sales professionals shy away from using the telephone as a strategic instrument that can be used to increase Suspect and Prospect contact. Most sales professionals seem to prefer to use the telephone for visiting, not for selling. Others avoid using the telephone for the majority of the day.

The telephone should be used to maximize selling time. Use the telephone to:

1. Reach out and introduce yourself and your offers.

2. Call people who have been referred to you by clients and Advocates.

3. Follow up during downtime and nonpresentation times with happy customers for additional opportunities.

4. Establish meeting times with Prospects and Customers.

5. Close sales.

Learn to recognize the time frames in each day that seem to be high-yielding contact times and low contact times; then coordinate your schedule accordingly. For example, if Monday mornings are difficult times to reach contacts (for whatever reason), then don't plan for Monday mornings to be heavy outbound calling times. If you keep a contact log (diary, database management system, personal calendar) with notations of individuals you have talked to earlier and who have requested a follow-up call on a specific date, then call resistance should not be an issue—you have set calls to be made for a purpose.

A common frustration for sales professionals is leaving or receiving telephone messages that seem vague and that leave one wondering exactly what to do next. In leaving a message for someone else (whether in an electronic voice system or with a person at the other end of the telephone), follow these guidelines:

1. Leave your name; spell it.

2. Leave your telephone number for follow-up; repeat it twice.

3. Leave an action-oriented message that tells the listener exactly what you want him to do.

4. Make sure your message indicates to the listener that there is some value to be realized from calling you back.

If you are leaving a message with a person, always start by politely asking the other person, "Do you have something to write with?" You will be amazed how many times the other person will respond to that question by saying, "Just a moment, let me get a pen." Make sure the message you leave is written down.

If you are leaving a message in someone's electronic voice mail system, consider standing up as you leave the message. This change in physiology makes your voice sound significantly firmer, more solid, and more energized!

Just as with face-to-face interactions, remember that sales professionals should always have a purpose for any conversation (Stacking-N-Linking Model, Mini-Seminar 11). Your telephone call is an interruption in the other person's life (unless the person specifically requested that you call, so the conversation must have a purpose. Once that purpose has been accomplished, end the call politely.

To maximize overall sales activities, learn to monitor your own daily account development activities to recognize what times during each day are best for placing and receiving calls. Consider working across time zones, if applicable; that strategy can allow a sales professional to maximize overall daily productivity.

Recognize that your ability to cultivate relationships with people over the telephone is essential for sales transactions. Getting the gatekeeper at the other end of the line to accept you may make the difference between getting through to the intended contact or merely leaving endless messages. Knowing others' voice mail system extension numbers allows you to reach out and leave action-oriented messages before and after traditional work hours.

Use the telephone to peak performance, arming yourself with the reference materials, files, computer access, and work space within easy reach of the telephone. Consider purchasing and using a cordless phone, a longer receiver cord, a headset, or a cellular phone.

Like it or not, the telephone is a powerful selling tool through which relationships can be developed and greater levels of efficiency attained.

Objective

1. To help participants recognize that the world of selling is not only a face-to-face activity in the new century.

Time Required

20–30 minutes

Materials Needed

- As many samples of technology as you can provide that is being used in sales in general or in your organization specifically

- One copy of the activity sheet for each participant

- A flip chart or whiteboard

Directions for the Trainer

1. Read the lecturette prior to your training session, and take notes so you can use it as the basis for your own comments to the group.

2. Start the training session by summarizing the lecturette in your own words; then pass out the activity sheets.

3. Activity Sheet 48-A: Have participants discuss how technology can be used to prospect more effectively and to stay in selling contact with customers. Ask several participants to share their diagrams, and discuss how each item can be used effectively.

Mini-Seminar 48

Using Other Forms of Technology to Complement Your Sales Effectiveness

LECTURETTE

The "good old boy" network of selling and relationships is gone from the new, fast-paced e-world. Understanding the new and evolving technologies and how to strategically use them in the daily selling world is essential for every sales professional.

Technology is evolving at such a fast pace that whatever technology plan one develops, it can realistically be outdated by implementation time. Your ability and willingness to be flexible are critical to the successful use of technology.

Technology can be found in many selling situations:

1. A sales professional is equipped with a portable data instrument that allows access to a database of information and communication options in the palm of one's hand.

2. Instant communication, updates, announcements, grams, and newsletters can be sent to e-mail addresses.

3. Communication, advertisement, awareness, order entry, registration, and subscriptions can be offered via an organization's website.

4. Laptop computers, portable printers, faxes, e-mail capabilities, and cellular phones enable a sales professional to telecommute and have a virtual office anywhere in the world.

5. Teleconferencing, satellite connections, and high-speed digital connections allow audio and video interaction from remote locations and allow individuals instant access to information that may otherwise have been unavailable to them.

6. Fax machines allow instant transmission of paper materials, eliminating time delays.

Technology is in a 100-meter dash today. Whatever technology you have, chances are good that someone else may have even more, greater, faster, and newer technology than you.

Sales professionals must recognize technology as a selling partner to be embraced and used effectively.

ACTIVITY 48-A
USING OTHER FORMS OF TECHNOLOGY TO COMPLEMENT YOUR SALES EFFECTIVENESS

PARTICIPANT'S HANDOUT

Diagram on this page or on a large wall chart how you can use and integrate all of the items listed (and any others you wish to add) to market your organization, product, or service offering.

Website

Fax machine

Database

Teleconferencing

Portable Data Instrument

E-mail addresses

Laptop computers

Cellular phones

Copyright McGraw-Hill 2001. Original purchasers of this book are permitted to photocopy or customize this page by downloading it from www.books.mcgraw-hill.com/training/download. The document can then be opened, edited, and printed using Microsoft Word or other word processing software.

Objective

1. To help participants maximize their daily work schedule for increased sales efficiency.

Time Required

20–30 minutes

Materials Needed

- Have all sales professionals bring with them whatever instrument or device they utilize on a daily basis to maintain control over their activities.

- One copy of the activity sheet for each participant

- A flip chart or whiteboard

Directions for the Trainer

1. Read the lecturette prior to your training session, and take notes so you can use it as the basis for your own comments to the group.

2. Start the training session by summarizing the lecturette in your own words; then pass out the activity sheets.

3. Activity Sheet 49-A: Have participants modify whatever existing time management device they use to incorporate the Quadrant Manager System for ten consecutive workdays. Next, have them develop a weekly marketing Quadrant Manager and a weekly selling Quadrant Manager. Then have participants pair off to discuss their plans for implementation.

Time Management Effectiveness with the Quadrant Manager System

LECTURETTE

Being active and being productive are worlds apart. Many sales professionals are very active and have a lot of activity going on around them daily, yet others seem to generate better bottom-line results. The reason is simple: Merely being active is not the same as being productive!

Managing time and having the self-discipline to stay focused are crucial to maximizing every precious moment for prospecting, customer contact, selling, marketing, and taking care of the administrative responsibilities associated with the act of selling.

To maximize your time, start by asking yourself three strategic questions to determine what activities should be scheduled at what time intervals each day:

1. As a sales professional, do you have your greatest overall daily energy in the morning or afternoon hours?

2. Within that defined window of time (if you're a morning person, that would be from whatever time your day starts through noon; if you're an afternoon person, that would be from noon through the typical hour you end each day), define the hours that constitute morning or afternoon notation.

3. Now within those hours, break out the precise hours when you feel that you are at your best and are at peak performance. This is your prime time.

Your greatest level of productivity occurs when only high-level, important activities take place within the peak performance times—your prime time.

With this calculated focus, now review whatever system you use to manage your daily work flow and ensure that no important task gets overlooked. Consider adapting that system to another technique to increase your effectiveness even more.

The Quadrant Manager System allows for a universal overview of one's work to be seen, planned, and monitored. The Quadrant Manager System allows for work to be managed not based on what one would like to get done, but based on what is important. Also, the system is powerful, as it keeps all important work areas moving forward at the same time. Every day, there are important things to do, people to call, people to see, and items that need to be completed or written.

There are three steps to using the Quadrant Manager System:

First, create the template that you will write into. To do so, simply draw a large plus sign.

Second, place entries into the template, a maximum of three entries per category.

Third, review items objectively and then prioritize. Place a 1 beside the most important item in each of the four quadrants created by the plus sign template. Then continue on with numbers 2 and 3 in each quadrant.

A Quadrant Manager System approach to managing the important tasks may be developed on a blank sheet of paper, modified, and added into a daily to-do list system or a daily work planner binder. The instrument can look like this:

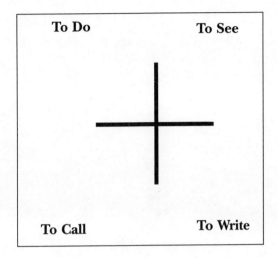

The Quadrant Manager System is an efficient tool for managing overall work responsibilities. With the top three important items noted in each quadrant daily, sales professionals can gauge when they are focusing on low-priority items, getting off track, or avoiding work.

Another powerful way to use the Quadrant Manager System to enhance selling effectiveness is to develop two additional and more specific Quadrant Managers for execution on a daily, weekly, or monthly basis.

1. **Develop a Marketing Quadrant Manager System** that outlines the top three items To Do, To Call, To See, and To Write that can feed the Sales Funnel from a marketing and prospecting aspect and lead to future selling opportunity contacts.

2. **Develop a Sales Quadrant Manager System** that would outline the top three items To Do, To Call, To See, and To Write that can immediately move you to a Close in the selling process.

Sales professionals must be great stewards of their professional time, and they must also think in specific terms of marketing and selling time responsibilities. The Quadrant Manager System powerfully addresses all three areas of responsibility.

ACTIVITY 49-A
TIME MANAGEMENT EFFECTIVENESS WITH
THE QUADRANT MANAGER SYSTEM

Diagram on this page the four time responsibility areas and then identify only the top three most important items for each area to attend to after this session.

Then develop a personal Marketing Quadrant Manager System and Selling Quadrant Manager System of action items that you can commit to for the next week.

Copyright McGraw-Hill 2001. Original purchasers of this book are permitted to photocopy or customize this page by downloading it from www.books.mcgraw-hill.com/training/download. The document can then be opened, edited, and printed using Microsoft Word or other word processing software.

Objectives

1. To introduce participants to the cutting-edge advantage of account management and development using an electronic data system.

2. To coach participants on how to manage, market, follow up, and stay in contact with their suspects, prospects, and customers more efficiently with a software database system.

Time Required

20–30 minutes

Materials Needed

- A sample of the database management system that your organization is using, or sample literature of market-ready software database management systems

- A flip chart or whiteboard

- An overhead projector and screen

- Template Master 50-A

Directions for the Trainer

1. Read the lecturette prior to your training session, and take notes so you can use it as the basis for your own comments to the group.

2. Start the training session by summarizing the lecturette in your own words; then display the database management template on the screen.

3. Activity 50-A: Discuss and answer questions about the database management system used by your organization.

Mini-Seminar 50

Using a Database Management System to Assist in Your Sales Efforts

LECTURETTE

Effective account management and development will make or break the sales professional's performance cycle.

Attempting to stay mentally aware of every account and the status of each one is an impossibility. However, with the utilization of an electronic account database system, that impossibility becomes a manageable daily reality.

Sales professionals must understand the necessity of managing all account activity with a database system. The market makes available a wide range of software options and vendor partnership possibilities. Selecting the right system for your computer is important. Some of the leading options are:

1. FileMaker Pro

2. GoldMine

3. ACT

4. Excel (custom-built system)

5. Lotus 1-2-3 (custom-built system)

Make sure that whatever system you choose, it has the power to deliver what you need now, the flexibility to be modified easily (and with limited or no additional costs) as your sales grow, and the capacity to be expanded as business needs grow and change.

The database system you use should allow you to store the following data points and therefore conduct searches accordingly.

1. **Register a date field** for follow-up or call-back, so that on that specific date your computer produces an automatic call report of individuals to be contacted, based upon previous notations made into the database.

2. **Code in each entry individually, based on their level of importance.** Code using numbers 1 through 4.

3. **Store personal contact data:**
   a. personal name
   b. address
   c. city
   d. state
   e. zip
   f. phone
   g. fax
   h. e-mail
   i. alternate telephones
   j. expandable notes section

4. **Store professional contact data:**

   a. organizational name

   b. title

   c. address

   d. city

   e. state

   f. zip

   g. phone (ideally a toll-free number)

   h. fax

   i. e-mail

   j. alternate telephones

   k. expandable notes section

The date field is important. Whenever a new account is added or you contact an account and that account indicates that you should follow up on a designated date, you can log that date into the date field section. Then, when the computer is turned on that date, a prepared list of contacts is made available to the sales professional for immediate action.

The client code section is also valuable; by placing a code value on every entry, a sales professional can do a database search at any time to determine the number of qualified contacts in any specific category. The code is also valuable in performing category-specific direct mailings, e-mail promotions, and fax marketing campaigns to suspects, prospects, or active clients. Use whatever coding system works for you; for example, a system of four numbers might represent:

Code 1 = a contact who has Money, Need, Date for acquisition of your offer.

Code 2 = a contact who meets two of the above three criteria.

Code 3 = a contact who meets one of the above three criteria.

Code 4 = a contact who doesn't meet any of the above three criteria, yet earns a position within the database (e.g., a person of influence over a criteria Code 1, 2, or 3 contact name; a family member or friend; someone who may not be a buying customer but serves a marketing or promotional purpose).

The database is also valuable because you can create your own notes section codes and, by maintaining some uniformity, search the notes section at any time for the volume of contacts with the same notes (e.g., "sent XYZ Promotional mailer" appearing in the note section of those contacts would allow you to produce a list of only those contacts).

The database is a life-sustaining component of the sales professional's organizational structure for today and tomorrow.

Home

Title | **First Name** | **MI** | **Last Name**

Address

City | **St.** | **ZIP Code**

Country

Follow up Date

Phone Type | **Phone Number**

E-Mail

Client Code Level:

Client ID #   JMI 102597

Sales Rep

Business

Name

Title

Address

City | **St.** | **ZIP Code**

Notes

Client ID #   JMI 102597

Sales Rep

Copyright McGraw-Hill 2001. Original purchasers of this book are permitted to photocopy or customize this page by downloading it from www.books.mcgraw-hill.com/training/download. The document can then be opened, edited, and printed using Microsoft Word or other word processing software.

Objective

1. To help participants understand their relationships with accounts and perform a competitive analysis based upon product, service, people, market competition, and levels of buyers and decision makers involved in every transaction.

Time Required

20–30 minutes

Materials Needed

- One copy of the activity sheet for each participant

- Have participants bring the profile information they have on their number one client and on a client they are in the Presentation phase with at the present time.

- A flip chart or whiteboard

- An overhead projector and screen

- Template Master 51-A.

Directions for the Trainer

1. Read the lecturette prior to your training session, and take notes so you can use it as the basis for your own comments to the group.

2. Start the training session by summarizing the lecturette in your own words; then pass out the activity sheets to each participant.

3. Activity Sheet 51-A: Facilitate a discussion on how to use the profile as a pre-sales-call refresher of a client's account status, and how to use it to trace account development activities.

Mini-Seminar 51

Tracking Your Account Activity and Status

LECTURETTE

The seasoned sales professional understands the significance of information. It's important to determine how much you know about any specific customer and to recognize any areas of information deficiency.

Recall a time when a sale was missed or lost due to a lack of knowledge about a customer, an incorrect point of contact, or a missed decision maker in the buying process. Conversely, recall a time when a sale was made because you had a specific piece of information about a customer that your competition lacked!

While some sales professionals maintain a mental flow chart of critical information points to obtain from a customer, many beginning and junior sales professionals miss this valuable step to sustained selling success.

Any thorough customer profile analysis form should focus questions in three areas:

1. **Actual account contact demographic data profile** (see Mini-Seminar 50).

2. **Background and historical profile data.**

3. **Performance profile questions concerning your relationship with the core decision makers** (see Mini-Seminar 19) and your position in relation to making a Close.

Use a tracking form like the one shown on the screen for accounts with multiple decision makers, or large product or service buyers for whom the buying process is a very involved activity. While a tracking form could be used for every account, there may be accounts for which using such a form could be overkill.

On the sample form, the first two sections include self-explanatory information points. In the third section, you are scoring your point of contact against the four decision makers, to ensure that no decision has been overlooked. This section also allows you to objectively recognize your Presentation position with this customer.

Using a contact performance profile form, you can determine where you are at any given time in respect to:

1. making a sale,

2. your relationship with the client,

3. your strength with the client in relation to competitors,

4. how loyal you are to the client (based upon the volume of knowledge you have) and how loyal the client is to you (based upon prior sales results).

Knowledge is power, and the positive application of knowledge in the sales process leads directly to sales profitability.

SP 3"

sales
CONTACT PERFORMANCE PROFILE

P¹ = CONTACT PROFILE

Organization/Firm Name: _____   Primary Contact Name: _____
Address: _____   Box/Mail Stop: _____
City: _____   State/Province: _____
Postal Code: _____   Telephone I: _____
Fax: _____   Telephone II: _____

Org./Firm Birthday: _____   Contact Birthday: _____
Primary Product/Service/Mission Statement: _____

Secondary Product/Service/Mission Statement: _____

# of Members/Employees: _____   Org./Firm Net Worth: _____
Previous Year Earnings/Budget: _____   Officers' Names: _____

P² = BACKGROUND PURPOSE PROFILE

Product/Solution presented: _____   Is there a prior relationship here: YES/NO   Competitor(s): _____
Date of last interaction: _____   Was the outcome a "Win/Win": YES/NO
My position on this is: Exclusive--Dominant--Shared--Below--Unknown   Their timing on this is: Urgent--Working on it--No rush--Unknown
Single objective here is: _____
Secondary objective is: _____
Psychological profile: _____
Why are they considering my...: _____
Have I identified all decision makers: YES/NO   Have I visited with each: YES/NO   Can I answer their needs: YES/NO
Have all levels of the decision loop agreed: YES/NO/UNKNOWN   Is there interest in my Product/Solution: YES/NO   Is there interest in my competition: YES/NO
Has a decision date been set: YES/NO   Am I using all networking resources: YES/NO   Have I asked for the order: YES/NO

P³ = PERFORMANCE PROFILE

TYPES of BUYERS (TB)	CURRENT POSITION (CP)	BUYERS INVOLVED	(TB) ✔	(CP)	NEXT STEP	WHO/WHEN/WHERE	ST.OP.'s ✔
F=Financial	G=Growth	1.					
T=Technical	T=Trouble	2.					
U=User	S=Stable	3.					
Co=Coordinator	OC=Over Confident	4.					
		5.					

Jeff Magee International ©

Make the use of a profile form a routine self-management activity.

ACTIVITY SHEET 51-A
TRACKING YOUR ACCOUNT ACTIVITY AND STATUS
USING THE SALES CONTACT PERFORMANCE PROFILE FORM

PARTICIPANT'S HANDOUT

SP³" sales
CONTACT PERFORMANCE PROFILE

P¹ = CONTACT PROFILE

Organization/Firm Name: _____   Primary Contact Name: _____
Address: _____   Box/Mail Stop: _____
City: _____   State/Province: _____
Postal Code: _____   Telephone I: _____
Fax: _____   Telephone II: _____

Org./Firm Birthday: _____   Contact Birthday: _____
Primary Product/Service/Mission Statement: _____

Secondary Product/Service/Mission Statement: _____

# of Members/Employees: _____   Org./Firm Net Worth: _____
Previous Year Earnings/Budget: _____   Officers' Names: _____

P² = BACKGROUND PURPOSE PROFILE

Product/Solution presented: _____   Is there a prior relationship here: YES/NO   Competitor(s): _____
Date of last interaction: _____   Was the outcome a "Win/Win": YES/NO
My position on this is: Exclusive--Dominant--Shared--Below--Unknown   Their timing on this is: Urgent--Working on it--No rush--Unknown
Single objective here is: _____
Secondary objective is: _____
Psychological profile: _____
Why are they considering my...: _____
Have I identified all decision makers: YES/NO   Have I visited with each: YES/NO   Can I answer their needs: YES/NO
Have all levels of the decision loop agreed: YES/NO/UNKNOWN   Is there interest in my Product/Solution: YES/NO   Is there interest in my competition: YES/NO
Has a decision date been set: YES/NO   Am I using all networking resources: YES/NO   Have I asked for the order: YES/NO

P³ = PERFORMANCE PROFILE

TYPES of BUYERS (TB)	CURRENT POSITION (CP)	BUYERS INVOLVED	(TB)✔ (CP)	NEXT STEP	WHO/WHEN/WHERE	S.T.O.P.'s ✔
F=Financial	G=Growth	1.				
T=Technical	T=Trouble	2.				
U=User	S=Stable	3.				
C=Cheerleader	OC=Over Confident	4.				
		5.				

Jeff Magee International ©

Copyright McGraw-Hill 2001. Original purchasers of this book are permitted to photocopy or customize this page by downloading it from www.books.mcgraw-hill.com/training/download. The document can then be opened, edited, and printed using Microsoft Word or other word processing software.

Objective

1. To help participants view their vocation as a profession and therefore conduct their ongoing activities, pursuits, and self-development in a professional manner.

Time Required

15–20 minutes

Materials Needed

- One copy of the activity sheet for each participant

- Have participants bring copies of their resumes or a listing of their educational, certification, and competency accomplishments

- A flip chart or whiteboard

Directions for the Trainer

1. Read the lecturette prior to your training session, and take notes so you can use it as the basis for your own comments to the group.

2. Start the training session by summarizing the lecturette in your own words; then pass out the activity sheets to each participant.

3. Activity Sheet 52-A: Facilitate a discussion on how participants measure other industries' professionals. Discuss how sales professionals see themselves and measure themselves.

Mini-Seminar 52

Becoming an Expert

LECTURETTE

How individuals measure other adults within the industries they represent and the standards used to differentiate a professional from someone who is merely working within the industry are typically very specific.

Ask yourself these questions:

1. If you were to choose a doctor to go to or to take your mother to, what credentials or certifications would you expect as a minimum in making your selection?

2. If you needed legal advice, who would you turn to? Why? How would you measure whether he or she were the appropriate person to talk to if you were standing in that person's office (place of business)?

3. If you needed assistance in preparing your income tax filings, whom would you go to? Why? How would you measure if he or she were the appropriate person to go to?

Here are some interesting answers:

1. Doctor = legitimate medical school; years of practice; license to practice; up on current trends, procedures, and medicines; certified credentials or diplomas on wall; current journals on the specialist's discipline in evidence; required to attend ongoing schooling to maintain the ability to do the job.

2. Lawyer = legitimate law school; years of practice; license to practice; up on current trends, procedures, and court rulings; certified credentials or diplomas on wall; current law journals in evidence; required to attend ongoing schooling to maintain the ability to do the job.

3. Accountant = legitimate school; years of practice; license to practice; up on current trends, procedures, and laws; certified credentials or diplomas on wall; current accounting or tax journals in evidence; required to attend ongoing schooling to maintain the ability to do the job.

Sales professionals need to treat their business with the same expectations people hold other high professions to. A doctor earns an M.D. and does what it takes to continuously maintain it; an attorney earns a J.D., passes the bar exam, and does what it takes to maintain licensure; an accountant earns a C.P.A. and does what it takes to maintain it.

As a sales professional in the industry you represent, so too should you continually endeavor to earn all appropriate certifications and credentials. That differentiates you from being merely another salesperson. A sales professional treats his or her profession just as doctors, lawyers, and accountants do theirs.

Sales professionals can be identified by their activities and accomplishments.

1. They seek out certification processes and accreditation in the industry they work in.

2. They attend regular education seminars, workshops, on-line courses, and teleconferences on what they do in an attempt to bring greater value to those they serve.

3. They subscribe to trade journals and publications to increase their learning curve and awareness of current trends and issues.

4. They participate in professional associations and clubs relevant both to selling and to the industry they represent.

5. They write for newsletters, journals, and trade publications within their industry for both internal consumption and customer readership.

6. They are avid readers about the industry and about selling.

ACTIVITY 52-A
BECOMING AN EXPERT:
PROFESSIONAL POSITION SURVEY QUESTIONNAIRE

Take a minute to complete this Professional Position Survey Questionnaire to determine your marketable advantages in the selling marketplace. Take stock of what you have to offer and what else you could be doing to elevate your level of sales professionalism.

1. Highest level of education: _____

2. Last industry-specific article written: _____

3. Last educational seminar or workshop or presentation given on behalf of my industry:_____

_____

4. Last educational seminar or workshop or presentation given on behalf of my organization: _____

_____

5. Certifications relating to selling: _____

6. Certifications relating to my product line: _____

_____

7. Certifications relating to services my organization offers: _____

_____

8. Certifications relating to anything else: _____

9. Last industry-specific conference attended: _____

10. Last educationally accredited seminar attended (CEU, CPE, CE): _____

_____

11. Last time someone referred to you as the subject-matter expert in your organization: _____

_____

12. The next training class you have scheduled on your own behalf that relates to your product or

service line offered: _____

13. The next training class you have scheduled on your own behalf that relates to your industry or

organization: _____

14. The number of industry-specific journals you regularly read: _____

_____

Copyright McGraw-Hill 2001. Original purchasers of this book are permitted to photocopy or customize this page by downloading it from www.books.mcgraw-hill.com/training/download. The document can then be opened, edited, and printed using Microsoft Word or other word processing software.

Professional Sales Skills Self-Assessment Inventory

The purpose of this inventory is to enable you to assess your present skill and knowledge levels in the science and art of selling. If you cannot answer any question, consider it a reflection of learning opportunities within this handbook. Each question relates to a specific skill set that is presented as a mini-seminar.

1. If someone were to ask you what you do or what you offer, can you respond in such a way that your statement is concise, solicits a follow-up opportunity from the other person, and does so in a matter of 20 seconds or less (Mini-Seminar 1)? Yes/No

2. Studies and research reveal that the sales process involves specific steps. Did you know this (Mini-Seminars 3 through 10)? Yes/No

3. What do you believe those specific steps to be (Mini-Seminars 3 through 10)?

4. What is a Suspect in the sales process (Mini-Seminar 14)?

5. What is a Prospect in the sales process (Mini-Seminar 14)?

6. What is a Customer in the sales process (Mini-Seminar 14)?

7. What is a Profile Customer (Mini-Seminar 15)?

8. What is a Qualified Suspect Profile (Mini-Seminar 16)?

9. What are the four core mental decisions made in any purchasing transaction (Mini-Seminar 19)?

10. Do you adjust your selling approach based on the generational segmentation you are interacting with (Mini-Seminar 21)? Yes/No

11. What is a definition of a Unique Selling Feature (Mini-Seminar 26)?

12. What is a definition of a Unique Service Feature (Mini-Seminar 27)?

13. Does customer service play a factor in sales (Mini-Seminar 40)? Yes/No

14. Is follow-up after the sale important (Mini-Seminar 42)? Yes/No

15. What should be printed on the reverse of your business card? How can you utilize the back of your business card as a selling tool (Mini-Seminar 44)?

16. What is an Advocate (Mini-Seminar 46)?

17. Do you feel comfortable using the telephone as a component of the sales process (Mini-Seminar 47)? Yes/No

18. Do you use different forms of technology, and, if so, which ones (Mini-Seminar 48)? Yes/No

19. How do you manage your contact names? Do you use an electronic database management system (Mini-Seminar 50)? Yes/No

20. Do you feel that you are an expert at what you do within your industry (Mini-Seminar 52)? Yes/No

Bibliography and Suggested Readings

Establishing a professional skill advantage in today's workplace requires continuous learning as well as knowledge application. Here are additional tools for sharpening your mental edge.

Advancing in Your Career, Jeff Magee, JM Publications, 1999.

Conceptual Selling, Robert B. Miller and Stephen E. Heiman, Warner Books, 1987.

Getting Past No, William Ury, Bantam Trade Paperback, 1993.

How to Close Every Sale, Joe Girard, Warner Books, 1989.

Sales Karate, John E. Richters, 1973.

Secrets of Closing Sales, Charles B. Roth and Roy Alexander, Prentice Hall, 1983.

Selling to VITO, the Very Important Top Officer, Anthony Parinello, Bob Adams Books, 1994.

Strategic Selling, Robert B. Miller and Stephen E. Heiman, Warner Books, 1985.

Success through a Positive Mental Attitude, Napolean Hill and W. Clement Stone, Pocket Books, 1960, 1977.

The Amazing Results of Positive Thinking, Norman Vincent Peale, Fawcett Crest Books, 1959, 1990.

The First Five Minutes, Norman King, Prentice Hall, 1987.

The New Strategic Selling, Stephen E. Heiman and Diane Sanchez with Tad Tuleja, Warner Books, 1998.

About the Author

Jeffrey L. Magee, Ph.D., PDM, CSP, CMC

Having started his first business in high school, Jeff sold the business to a major telephone book publishing company before leaving for college. Two years after graduating from college, Jeff was recognized by American Home Products as its leading sales professional in America, and participated in the national redesign team working on how sales associates' and territory managers' sales training indoctrination would take place. One year later, he experienced corporate downsizing.

Applying his sales knowledge, Jeff secured a position with a leading Midwest advertising agency within 24 hours of being downsized. He was quickly promoted to vice president, and participated in growing that business from $1.5 million to $15 million in annual bookings. During that same time period, Jeff became the youngest internationally certified sales instructor for the Dale Carnegie Sales Course.

Today, Dr. Jeff Magee is a Certified Management Consultant, Certified Speaking Professional, and Certified Professional Direct Marketer. Through his residential training and publishing business (Jeff Magee International, www.JeffreyMagee.com or 877-90-magee) and his web-based business (Warehouse:Intellect), he "works with the leading sales professionals and managers internationally who want cutting-edge, flexible training and learning solutions so they can stay ahead of the competition."

NOTES

NOTES

NOTES

NOTES

NOTES

NOTES

NOTES

NOTES

NOTES

NOTES

NOTES

NOTES